THE
Three
COMMITMENTS
of
LEADERSHIP

How Clarity, Stability, and Rhythm
CREATE GREAT LEADERS

TOM ENDERSBE • JAY THERRIEN • JON WORTMANN

New York Chicago San Francisco Lisbon London Madrid Mexico City
Milan New Delhi San Juan Seoul Singapore Sydney Toronto

1 2 3 4 5 6 7 8 9 10   DOC/DOC   1 6 5 4 3 2 1

ISBN   978-0-07-177459-8
MHID   0-07-177459-9

e-ISBN   978-0-07-177525-0
e-MHID   0-07-177525-0

McGraw-Hill books are available at special quantity discounts to use as premiums and sales promotions, or for use in corporate training programs. To contact a representative, please e-mail us at bulksales@mcgraw-hill.com.

This book is printed on acid-free paper.

To our wives, parents, and children.

CONTENTS

ACKNOWLEDGMENTS   IX

PREFACE   XI

CHAPTER 1   WHAT KIND OF LEADER DO YOU
WANT TO BE?   1
The Ship Is Sinking   1
Leaders Create New Realities   8
How We Learn to Be Leaders   13
You Can Be a Better Leader Right Now   15
The Other Jack   20
What Kind of Leader Do You Want
to Be?   33

CHAPTER 2   CLARITY   35
What Is the Commitment to Clarity?   35
Blind Men Baking Bread   38
Do You Have Clarity?   39
Dead Men Tell No Tales   42
Add, Keep, Delete   45
We Think We've Been Clear   48

The Sponge and Shortcuts 50
Asking Why 54
Puzzle Pieces 56
End Every Conversation with a Reframe 65
Simple Assessments: What Does Success
   Look Like? 66

CHAPTER 3   STABILITY 69
What Is the Commitment to Stability? 69
Starting Up a Culture of Stability 72
Do You Have Stability? 75
The *Nimrod* 76
Radar and the Alarm 83
Recognize Each Teammate's
   Fear Response 84
Free Lunch, No Chores, Unlimited
   Learning, and Consistent Messages 86
General Mills 91
Why Trust Is Essential for Stability 94
How to Create a Culture of Trust 96
What to Do with Emotion 102
Simple Assessments: What Do
   You Need? 105

CHAPTER 4   RHYTHM 109
What Is the Commitment to Rhythm? 109
The Perfect Work Day 113
Do You Have Rhythm? 116
Henry Ford on Thomas Edison 118
The Foundation of Rhythm Is Freedom 123
Happiness Equals Rhythm 124
Regular Measurement 127
Weekly Reviews 134

Renewing Rituals   136
Simple Assessments: What's in
   Your Way?   139

CHAPTER 5   HOW TO BUILD A TEAM OF
            LEADERS   141
            The Greatest Scientist Whose Name We
               Don't Remember   141
            The Problem with Opportunities   144
            What Is a Team of Leaders?   147
            The Elephant Approach   149
            How to Assess When Someone's Ready
               to Lead   154
            First Ask Why   156
            The Ways to Build Confident Leaders   159
            Our Teams of Leaders Are All
               Around Us   162
            What Leaders Crave   165

CHAPTER 6   1,000,000 LEADERS   167
            A World of Leaders   167
            Kissing Your Enemy   168
            The Math   170
            The Musician's Village   172
            Leaders for Life   174
            A Community of Aspiration   177
            The Inevitable Doubt   180
            Lead Every Day   182
            Postlude: The Unexpected Prize   184

SELECTED BIBLIOGRAPHY   187
INDEX   189

ACKNOWLEDGMENTS

The leaders who taught us, who made us want to be leaders too, began our development that led to this book. We are grateful to our mentors, teachers, and teammates: Bob Bachelder, Jon Banas, Stacy Brusa, Bob Endersbe, Jim Flynn, Josh Grzelak, Claudia Highbaugh, Doug Lennick, Joe Mayher, Thirb Millott, Steve Palen, Aldo Sicoli, Kathleen Stone, and Kathi Whitmore.

Thank you to Mark Bryan, author of the *Artist's Way at Work*, for his coaching; to our agent, Giles Anderson, for his unfaltering faith and guidance; to our editor, Knox Huston, for his constant encouragement and belief in the book's ideas, and Webster Williams and Maureen B. Dennehy for their superior editing.

As a writing team, we are grateful to the many readers whose insight improved the final work: Brian Ahearn, Larry Campion, Janet Cataldo, Tim Clark, Rusty Field, Jesse Heise, Heather Margolis, Peter Martin, Maria Olson, Jennifer Peterson, Tim Ruggles, Kai Sakstrup, Matt Trottier, Robert Wortmann, and Brian Zanghi.

PREFACE

We know you're busy. We also know you picked up this book because you want to be a better leader. That's why we've distilled our leadership model into three words that you can never forget: *clarity*, *stability*, and *rhythm*. Whether we're dealing with a crisis or working day-to-day to run a team or organization, when we lead, each of us needs a sticky and straightforward way of practicing leadership so we always know what to do. Equally as important: we need a method that turns us into the kind of leaders people beg to work with.

These three words will become not only the core of how you lead but your guideposts in the most difficult moments to overcome the challenges that sink most leaders. Open the three commitments, learn what they are, and when you feel the inevitable worry and fear that accompanies leadership—from leading in a multinational corporation to your child's sports team—you will know how to inspire and connect with your team, and produce better outcomes together.

How we lead needs to be simple. Everyone is capable of leading, and many of the leaders whose impact we remember have taken a minimalist and no-nonsense approach to how they lead. Discovering the core of what they did will allow you to instantly have an affect on the places your work matters the most.

Notice, though, that we said how we lead needs to be simple—not that it needs to be easy. Too many leadership resources confuse the simplicity of leadership with the reality that leading is extremely difficult. Becoming a leader others respect and want to work with takes years of intentional learning and practice, but that's not how most leadership resources teach. Instead of providing us with a memorable, immediately applicable model, they ask us to learn 50 rules, follow 14-step plans, and apply 16 box matrices.

Most adult brains cannot commit the rules and steps to memory quickly. To compound the problem, if we make the time to remember the models, in our busyness we run out of time before we practice them. The most overlooked fact with any learning event is that if the lessons are not put into practice within 48 hours, the information will not stick. The majority of leadership training used by organizations across the globe doesn't apply to the problems we're facing today, and the complexity of the models each training presents distracts us from what we truly need when we're leading: a way of thinking that concentrates everything we *do* so our leadership has a direct and measurable affect.

We've written *The Three Commitments* so you can apply them after reading the opening pages; and we've designed it for your busy life. The mantra of *The Three Commitments* is: pay attention. Each chapter is like a little book providing the insight you need to feel in control during the trials that test all leaders. Once you've completed each chapter, you will know compelling ways to improve how you work with the people you lead. And each chapter will take you deeper toward the ultimate goal of the book: building a team of leaders.

The first chapter is a primer on all three commitments. Before introducing what the commitments are and why they matter, we begin with a vivid account of how they can be applied in the most dire leadership moments; the chapter concludes with a case study about using the three commitments to overcome one of the most irritating problems for every leader. The next three chapters break down each commitment in detail so that once you understand them, you can begin practicing them with your team. We'll tell you stories of history's giants who have fulfilled the commitments, profile organizations that apply the commitments every day, and offer ways you can use the commitments as a leader in any setting.

The final two chapters reveal both the full potential of the model and our dream. Chapter 5 teaches how you can build a team of leaders. Not only do we want you to be an effective leader, we also want you to create a culture where how you lead develops every person you work with into a leader too. None of us want to bear the burden of leadership alone. The responsibility is too heavy, and none of us by ourselves are as valuable as a team that loves working together. Then, in the final chapter, we offer a plan to create a world of leaders. What if every kindergartener was taught simple ways to be an effective leader? This book is not only about making you the leader you want to be; it's about how by paying attention to three commitments, as a world of leaders we can take on the greatest challenges facing our planet in the twenty-first century and beyond.

CHAPTER 1

WHAT KIND OF LEADER DO YOU WANT TO BE?

The Ship Is Sinking

The sky is a blanket of black. It's 2:30 a.m, and the moon has set; the stars barely light the few feet in front of him. The skipper can barely see the other twelve men on the boat. There are two other boats patrolling with his: they're ghosts, trying to ambush the enemy. This is the passage their destroyers sail as they return home from battle.

One of the other officers is on the bow. He's using his binoculars, scanning the dark to locate a target. The 80-foot motor torpedo boat is the perfect surprise weapon, faster and smaller than the enemy's giant ships. The skipper is at the wheel, waiting. He has a quick daydream about sailing as a child. He's always loved the sea. The skipper snaps back to attention, and he thinks he sees his fellow officer point. His skin tingles at the prospect of action.

Then the scout bellows, "Ship at two o'clock!"

Because the skipper is trying to prevent detection, only one of the boat's three engines is fired up. He spins the wheel, hard; but it's sluggish. The boat crawls. The night is so quiet, but suddenly he sees a 379½-foot enemy destroyer, towering 60 feet high and approaching at 40 knots. He doesn't have time to hear the roar.

In the next moment, the skipper's boat is split in half. The only thing visible are the flames from gasoline burning on the water's surface. Frantically, he scans the scene. Men were thrown from the boat, and the boat's wake spread them over an area larger than a football field. Some of them are hurt, and others can't swim—their life vests barely keep them afloat. They scream for help. The skipper and four others are still on the bobbing hull, and he realizes the current is pushing the fire toward them. Because he is the commander of a sinking ship, his men's lives depend on what he does next.

This vignette is a true story. Leadership experiment Number One: what would you do? Your ship is sinking; men are in the water, hurt and screaming; burning gasoline is about to overtake the only part of your boat that's floating; and five of you are in its path. What's the first action you'd take? If you're hesitating, imagine. Imagine yourself on half a boat. It's pitch-black. You have crew in the water. Feel the fear and tension of that moment. And feel the weight. Those men need you, and you have the courage and the strength to help them.

There is no wrong answer to this question, just like there's no perfect way to lead. The three commitments we'll teach you will focus your attention as a leader whether you're directive or collaborative, in a strict hierarchy or a flat model. Each of us is different in our leadership style: what matters is who was included in your answer. If you thought, *jump in the water*, you're right, but did you say anything to the other four men who were with you?

When a ship is sinking—whether it's a business, a government, or a city or region facing a natural disaster—the first, completely understandable human instinct is to save yourself. Leaders want to save themselves too; this book is not about martyrdom, even though self-sacrifice is essential for leadership. The three commitments are about making sure our people always have what they need to thrive. The leaders we revere and the ones that get results, *they pay attention*: to how they lead, to the environment their leadership creates and to every person on their team.

In the actual story, the skipper's first action was to yell, "Over the side." He gave clear instructions that focused those around him, and when the destroyer's wake moved the floating fire away from the boat's remains, they climbed back aboard. Then he took account of his situation. He had four men on the boat with him and another eight in the water, at least a few of them seriously injured and begging for help.

Again, he was *clear*. He wanted to know exactly who was still with him, so he had every man call out his name. Of the 12 men, 10 were accounted for. Next, he told one of his men to blink a light so the healthy could swim to the boat. Then, pinpointing the direction from which one of the wounded was yelling, he took off his clothes and dove into the water. Over the next three hours, before the sun rose, he and those who were still healthy got every man onto what was left of the ship.

As dawn began to break, the men were scared. The skipper, of course, was scared too. He didn't want to be in the middle of a disaster, but he was ready for it: he didn't become the commander of that boat by accident. He wanted to lead. He used his connections to get into the war early. He didn't want to sit on the sidelines, and he ended up in the Pacific theater during its most perilous time.

What he was doing for his men began when he was young. He was a Boy Scout. He ran organizations in high school, both official and the playful Muckers Club known for pulling practical jokes throughout the campus. He led drama and athletic teams in college—his captainship of the swimming team had been of particular importance when his men were in the water. He traveled the world, and his first book about leadership and foreign affairs had been published and become a bestseller the month after he graduated. When he found himself shipwrecked with men in the water, he had been preparing for this moment his entire life.

By the time he and the able-bodied tended to the wounded, the sun was rising. They were still on the remaining half of the boat, and in the distance, they could see numerous islands; they knew the enemy occupied all of them. They started to argue. There was nothing in their military training to prepare them for this. There wasn't enough room for all of them on the boat; the wounded needed the space, so the skipper took over. He had to rebuild their trust in one another and create some kind of *stability* in the chaos if they were going to survive. Except for the two hurt seamen, he ordered everyone including himself into the shark-infested water. They spent the morning watching for enemy planes, shocked that no one had come to their rescue.

Then, at 10 a.m., their injured vessel began to creak—even the wounded men had to get in the dark water and hang on. The boat capsized, guaranteeing it would sink, and the skipper made the decision most people would have thought was insane. The men who could swim grabbed a piece of the boat's timber and headed for the one island that, while further away, they bet was too small to be occupied. The skipper then cut one of the straps on the life vest of a man who was burned too badly to move. He put the strap in his own mouth, and began to swim. Every few minutes he would stop and rest and talk with the man in tow. It took five hours to reach the island, but everyone made it safely.

The stability of dry land, however, wasn't enough. To be rescued, they had to draw the attention of a passing friendly ship without attracting the enemy. That meant preserving their energy as long as it took. The skipper helped them find an uncomfortable but necessary *rhythm*. Each day, he or one of his men or sometimes the two together, would swim out into the boat passage where they were most likely to be found. The others laid low: they watched dogfights in the sky, ate the coconuts that had fallen, and tried to keep their spirits up.

After four days, the skipper changed the plans. He knew they needed water and hope. He took the strongest man and swam with him an hour to the closest island. Reaching the beach, they saw one of the enemy's shipwrecked barges, and two men. The two men saw them but jumped in their canoe and paddled away. The skipper and his man crept up on the barge and found what they needed: hardtack, water, and a small native canoe, which was big enough for only one man.

All day, they hid from the enemy and tried to explore the island. When night fell, the skipper left his mate and paddled back to the other men and delivered the rations. His crew told him that the two men he had seen during the day were actually natives of the local islands: they had visited and described where the Japanese were and how to avoid them. The next morning, the skipper headed back toward the island where they had found the food and he had left his mate.

But on the way, a strong wind arose. The waves were too big for him to prevent water from pouring into his canoe. In minutes, he was swamped. The canoe sank from under him, and he was alone in the water. After five days, almost dying at least twice, the skipper felt as though he couldn't escape this time. He imagined home and the bay where he swam as a child. He remembered an image of being under rough water, the sun pouring through, and how calm he felt. He thought of his men. He wondered whether he had prepared them; if they would get home.

There will be moments, even when you've done everything right, that everything goes wrong. This is another reason why the three commitments are so vital. When you commit to the experience you want your teammates to have when they work with you, they notice. They absorb the way you speak and think; they model the behaviors you use because they are effective. The three commitments show leadership that people want to learn and that gets results, even if you never intentionally try to develop your teammates into leaders. If you follow the three commitments, when it looks as if everything is falling apart, you have a team of leaders ready to step up and keep the important work you do together.

We need others to help us reach any goal. As the skipper thought about dying, out of nowhere another canoe of natives appeared. They pulled him out of the waves and brought him to the island with the barge. They showed him where another two-man canoe was stored. Before they left, the skipper took out his knife and scratched a message on a coconut for the natives to deliver, praying it would find its way to his commanders: "NAURO ISL COMMANDER KNOWS POSIT HE CAN PILOT 11 ALIVE NEED SMALL BOAT KENNEDY."

The skipper, a young John F. Kennedy, knew what to do under pressure, and that's what the three commitments do every time we get the privilege of leading: they reveal what to pay attention to so our teams never forget that what they're trying to accomplish is worth the fight. Kennedy's crew could have given up so many times. They could have missed the slim chances they had at life in the fear and real danger that surrounded them. Instead, he focused their energy, helped them feel secure and united, and generated a flow of effort that had only one purpose: getting home—and they did.

The natives who saved JFK had been working with the New Zealand Army. They had taken the message on the coconut to their contact and returned the next day with a stove and food for the men, and a letter for Kennedy. It read:

On His Majesty's Service.
To Senior Officer Kennedy, Naru Island.

I have just learned of your presence on Nauru Is. I am in command of a New Zealand infantry patrol operating in conjunction with U.S. Army troops on New Georgia. I strongly advise that you come with these natives to me. Meanwhile I shall be in radio communication with your authorities at Rendova, and we can finalize plans to collect balance of your party. Lt. Wincote.

P.S. Will warn aviation of your crossing Ferguson Passage.

After surviving the sinking of his ship, Kennedy stayed in the war until 1945. His back was never the same after pulling his injured crewman five hours to safety. What never changed was his commitment to a way of leadership that helped him become the thirty-fifth president of the United States.

Before we dig into what the commitments are, a quick note on the examples we're using throughout the book. We are not intending to hold up Kennedy or any of the other individuals we highlight as the ideal leader. The criticisms of how Kennedy and his men ended up in the destroyer's path, fact or fiction, point to possible failures in leadership. As a human being, Kennedy had the same kind of weaknesses that live in most of us. There simply is no perfect leader, and we hope that inspires you. We hope it takes away some of the false perceptions of who can be a leader. No matter what your background, education, or present place in life, you can lead too.

What we're emphasizing in this book is what leaders do in the moments that matter most and how they arrived at those moments: the way they prepared and practiced. We will hold up and examine what was eternally valuable about the thinking and actions of the leaders who so many of us admire. We will focus on how they led at their best in a way that shows how you can make the same commitments as they did. Great leadership is actually quite simple; we just need to know where to put our attention.

Leaders Create New Realities

Leadership is the act of creating new realities. And every leader knows deeply that creating new realities is grueling. No part of leadership is ever easy, but when the pressure rises and you know what to do, leadership can be the most rewarding experience in life. Conversely, when we don't know what to do, leadership can be one of the most frustrating and painful experiences most people never want to repeat. There is nothing worse than being in the leader's seat, with all eyes on you, and you feel helpless. We've been there, but by applying the three commitments, we hope to save each of us from ever having that experience again. The three commitments that make you the kind of leader people love to work with are clarity, stability, and rhythm.

When these three words become the focus of how you lead, you will always feel ready to act. In fact, when they become muscle memory—out of which you confront the daily challenges of developing a team who wants to work together and during moments of crisis when you need to take command— leading may even feel like what you were always supposed to do. Why are they commitments? They are the three realities that every human being needs each day to engage with their work while deeply valuing the experience.

The first commitment is *clarity*. Clarity is total awareness about the core knowledge of what we do, in ourselves and in every member of our team. If it sounds elementary, it is; too often as leaders, however, we have an ineffective habit when sharing information: we want to tell someone to do something once and then have it done. That, in and of itself, is not clarity. Dictating instructions and expecting performance can still work in such hierarchical environments as the military. But even if you have stars on your shoulder, they won't value your leadership if you're not willing to seek to understand who your people are and what *they* need to be completely clear about in where they're going and in what you're doing together. They will not freely and enthusiastically continue to follow you into the trenches.

Committing to clarity starts when we develop a personal state of total awareness: of where we're going, what we need to get there, and why it matters. It is the first commitment because so many problems are instantly improved when we pay attention to where we're confused. Clarity is also the process of creating mutual understanding with every member of our team. What is the biggest issue facing your team right now? Is everyone involved 100 percent clear on the where, what, and why of the action required? We can't ever ignore the minor details or assume that everyone absorbed the exact meaning of every conversation, meeting, or e-mail.

True clarity happens in a group when every teammate knows what success looks like and has the confidence and the capacity to talk about it. We promised you could begin to apply the commitments after the opening pages. Where is your team underperforming? It is probably because some part of "what" they need to do, "why" it matters, or "how" to do it is unclear, and you can work on that immediately just by having a conversation about where they're lacking clarity.

The second commitment, *stability*, is the promise to do everything we can so that everyone on our team or in our organization has what they need. To be successful consistently, each of us needs two things to feel stable: resources and a culture of trust. By resources, we mean everything from food and a safe place to work to tactical drills and coaching around the core skills of a person's role. With stability, we can take risks—share new ideas, collaborate, put in the extra time—and believe the effort will be worth it.

But risk taking happens only when we trust the people with whom we work and the organizations in which we serve. In our busyness and fatigue, leaders and organizations are too often inconsistent, disconnected, and unavailable. Now even though we don't mean to act this way, these behaviors destroy culture and create an environment of stagnation and underperformance.

Think about it right now: where is your team playing it safe? They can't take risks when they don't have the stability to jump. Even if your teammates have enough stability to keep up what they're doing today, will flat growth and no improvement in their performance get you closer to the new realities you want to create? We can immediately begin the process of building a stable environment by asking each person what he or she needs to feel stable. In many cases, what is required may be free and something you can provide easily.

The third commitment, *rhythm*, is a pattern that leaders foster to produce more of the results we want. In sports, rhythm is the zone. In business, it's peak performance—not just maximum efficiency but a place of heightened creativity and meaningful work as well. In psychology, it's described as flow. Leaders have incredible power to create an environment that innately removes the roadblocks that get in the way of people performing at their best. Even more important, as we achieve with our teams, we can pay attention to whether they're happy and whole.

When we are grounded as people and we feel that our efforts are part of a collective endeavor to do something important, we charge an environment with an energy and desire for excellence and progress. The commitment to rhythm—whether we do it through building efficiency, creativity, or that elusive place where everything just seems to work naturally (we'll go into detail about that holy grail of the three commitments in Chapter 4)—is how we raise the rate, volume, and quality of the work we and our teams produce.

Committing to rhythm has an unexpected benefit too: it causes our teams to love the work we're doing together. The simplest way to think about rhythm is to ask yourself where your people get stuck. It's happening because they do not have rhythm in what they do, as individual contributors and as a team. Ask them what's stopping their best efforts and you'll know what you need to do as their leader to produce better results.

We created the three commitments because we know each of us can be the kind of leader people respect and want to emulate. People will still follow the leaders whom they detest, but not for long. They may follow them because they have to— because they control their paycheck or because they have a position of authority—but they won't want to work with those leaders. In the French Revolution, the leaders whom people didn't want to follow were sent to the guillotine. In some countries, citizens still kill the leaders who fail them.

That's not going to happen to us at work. That's not going to happen when we can't balance the budget of our town as an elected official. We know our children's sports team will not rise up in armed revolt if we yell at them rather than nurture their talent. But when we lead poorly, the people around us stop working. In the office, they will start looking for new jobs and do only the minimum. In our community, they will move against us. The team, even a team of kids, will stop showing up. The three commitments are how we lead, no matter what we're trying to accomplish, so the people around us want to be on our team.

How We Learn to Be Leaders

Leaders are not born. Even though we've been trained to believe that certain individuals, especially the tall ones, were made for their role, the art and science of leadership is learned. We learn to lead by making commitments and from the experience of keeping them. A commitment is a promise and a pledge that binds us to what we're trying to do. In leadership, a commitment is a declaration about what we'll pour all our energy into making happen, and in some circumstances, even give our lives for.

Wait. Did we just write "give our lives for"? That may not be explicitly what you signed up for when you took on a leadership role, but when you look at the impact of what stress and long hours do to us, it's what we do every day. We're giving our precious energy to something; your energy is your life. Wherever you're spending your time each day is what you're giving your life to, and we don't want you to waste a moment.

That's why whether you lead at work, in government, or in your community, we're not writing about simply becoming a leader who others follow; we're writing about leading teams and entire organizations in which we commit to a way of working together that unleashes every person's energy and talent. Too many leaders in every setting shut their teams down because they don't know how to lead. The reason: the commitments we now need to make as leaders are evolving.

Throughout history, leaders committed to causes: unity, independence, discovering new lands, fighting evil, or building organizations that reached noble goals. They committed to defending their countries or growing their businesses. The commitment to what needs changing still can have lasting impact, but in the chaos and complexity of our modern world, where each second another problem to solve or another need to fill flashes across technology that fits in our hand, *what* we are committed to will too often not be enough.

The energy behind a cause—elections, caring for those after the devastation of a hurricane or tsunami, or keeping an organization from closing—will wane as all of our attention is called to hotter issues buzzing in our pockets. For instance, a robbery happens a few doors down from your house, and you commit to making your neighborhood of 50 families safer. You call a meeting to discuss options, and the room fills; everyone is angry and ready to act. Then at the next meeting, it's only seven of you.

Your new team decides to canvas your neighbors, and when you get back together—five of you this time—you learn how diverse the people's feelings are: some are too afraid to act, some don't care, some don't know what to do, and some of your neighbors are, in fact, the ones who are making the neighborhood unsafe. All five of you show up at the next meeting and you decide to reach out to local officials, but they don't return your calls. You realize that if you plan to fulfill your commitment, just wanting to make the neighborhood safe is not enough.

This pattern of the cause not being enough is playing out in every arena where we have important work to do. At work, we put in more hours than at any point in human history. We're working harder, and yet we're not getting better results. To lead in a way that empowers our entire team to produce the results we all want, we can't focus only on results. To be the kind of leaders who people will give their lives to work with, in addition to what we commit to achieving, we must also focus on the *experience* we create for the people we lead.

In this century and those that follow, the kind of leadership that our communities, our businesses, and our world needs must become a new, intentional way of interacting. What a leader promises and who the leader is will no longer inspire us more than briefly; the way a leader works with a team day in and day out, his or her natural tendencies and reactions, especially when the pressure rises—that has the potential to inspire us for generations.

Each of us learns how to lead through the practice of leading, by staying committed to others through the inevitable challenges of building a team that actually wants to work together and produce results. We discover our skills the first time we try to lead, and in each new opportunity to mentor, motivate, and guide the people who trust us, we refine and renew how we think and act. As our world continues to become more interconnected and complicated, learning how to lead demands a simple, unforgettable model.

We've discovered that game-changing leaders whose teams will follow them anywhere commit to more than just the goal; they commit to generating clarity, stability, and rhythm in everything they do. These three words are what we focus on in times of chaos so people have the grounding they need to survive. They are what we pay attention to every day with our teams and organizations so we foster an environment where people love showing up to work with us and nothing gets in the way of what we want to achieve together.

You Can Be a Better Leader Right Now

Learning to lead is never finished; even the best leaders can grow and improve. Too often as leaders—understandably overwhelmed by the speed, volume, and gravity of our work—we react to each new crisis rather than constantly preparing to adapt to our ever-changing new world. Despite the processes that are mapped on our walls and the detailed handbooks on our shelves, we do the first thing that comes to our minds. We react. Reaction, like Kennedy's after the destroyer attack, can be essential. But his reactions were a result of years of preparation.

Too often we react based on what's going to be best for us or what will solve the problem the quickest. Instead of being intentional about the way we lead, we do what's easiest. At first we often have the option to either do things with speed or accuracy; while we can initially only choose one, with time and practice both become possible. The three commitments provide a way of thinking about leadership that becomes the muscle memory of how we assess what needs to be done, act in a way that creates an environment of success, and teach others how to become leaders too.

Let's break down how you can apply the three commitments right now. The initial way to leverage the commitments is to use them as an *assessment* of your leadership or an environment where you're on a team. Think of the place where you lead. Ask yourself three questions:

1. Have I been clear?
2. Have I created stability?
3. Does our work have rhythm?

This is how you figure out what kind of leader you are today. In your definitions of a leader creating an environment that is clear, stable, and rhythmic, have you done so? If the answer is no to any of these questions, you begin to recognize the work you have to do. If the answer is sometimes, and that's the answer for many of us, the three commitments become a reminder of what great leaders need to pay attention to every day.

Now think of the commitments in a place where you are a teammate. Even if you're the CEO, you still don't run the board. In your personal life, even if you're the leader at work, you're the assistant coach of your child's softball team or a parent volunteer at school. In that environment:

- Is everything you need to know to be successful clear?
- Is there a stability that prevents fear, stress, and drama?
- Is there rhythm to the way people work together?

As an assessment, the commitments are a lens; they allow a team to truly see and determine where leadership is not creating the culture we need in order to be our best. Then instead of just filling out a form with numbers that go into a survey and gets lost in a drawer or the cloud, every one of us as teammates knows what to ask for so that our leaders can help us create the environment for success together. Want to know what kind of leader your people think you are? Ask them the three questions on the previous page. The commitments become the foundation of your reflection about what needs to be improved in your personal leadership and in the team or organization's work together.

The commitments can also be used to create an *action plan* that renews itself daily. Every time we present the commitments to a new group, each person in the room can describe what will create more clarity, stability, and rhythm for himself or herself and for the team. When that brainstorm is turned into a prioritized list of actions with responsible leaders and deadlines, meetings become the kind people want to attend;

instead of people talking about what we might do, we have a filter to decide what we *will* do—and quickly get to work. The process is as elementary as gathering the team and creating three lists of what is needed to have more clarity, stability, and rhythm; number each need in the order that will make the biggest impact. Instantly, you know what's missing in your work together and what to do about it.

For instance, in the example of making your neighborhood safer after a robbery, people stopped coming to the meetings because they had no reason to keep coming. After they expressed their feelings, they were satisfied and left the work of making the community safer to the organizers. If we wanted to keep more of our neighbors engaged, we could ask where people needed more clarity about how to stay safe, what would make the neighborhood feel more stable, and what rhythm of working together people could commit to. They would attend the next meetings because their questions would be answered (clarity), they could learn how to make a measurable difference in the neighborhood's safety (stability), and they chose the pattern of working together that fit into their life (rhythm). You can repeat the same process as a leader in any organization over a few meetings or as a regular exercise.

Finally, as you apply the three commitments—and this will feel like true magic—they are not only a way to analyze leadership and prioritize how to work more effectively together, but they also are the fundamental structure of a *development plan* to help others become leaders too. We don't really want to be the only leader on a team; the loneliness of the leader is a real symptom of taking responsibility. No one can understand what Atlas felt when he held the world on his shoulders more thoroughly than leaders who commit their entire person to what they do. There are days when we wonder if it's worth it, when the burdens others pile on us or the stress of what needs to be done feels so overwhelming we want to quit. It's in these moments that we have to remember we never need to lead alone.

We want a team of leaders, each responsible for outcomes that no one person can produce on their own. Can you imagine a team of leaders where every person can lead as well as you? When everyone can live the three commitments, we trust each teammate's ability to deliver on their promises. When conflict happens, and it will, we know that we're not the only one who can solve it. When we get stuck, a team of leaders is the engine that drives creative thinking and development. Instead of feeling like we have to come up with all the good ideas, we know that we have collaborative partners with whom we can discover the next opportunities and answers. We can all build teams of leaders, a team of people maximizing each other's potential to achieve, when we recognize that everyone has the capacity to lead.

The reason we too often lead alone, however, is that our teammates don't know how. Not knowing how to even begin fulfilling the leader's role stops them from ever putting their hand up when they have a brilliant idea or when a project emerges that they know they could lead well. Or, if they do have the courage to try and lead, when they face the initial and inevitable stress of being in charge, they may choke on the pressure and never try again.

That's a tragedy; the good news is, the three commitments fix it. When your people hear you talking about the three commitments, they'll learn the language, and start to notice what you do to lead effectively. When they see you creating clarity, stability, and rhythm, they'll recognize that producing extraordinary results doesn't have to be complicated, and they

will want to lead too. Leaders who make the three commitments continuously train their people to lead as well when
they model and encourage everyone to make the three commitments in all they do. The next example will show you how
to turn the theory of three commitments into a way of paying
attention to your people that they'll always remember.

The Other Jack

If we commit to creating an environment where teammates
have the clarity, stability, and rhythm they need to see that
their work results in something important, they will see it as
an experience they actually want to have. Most people work
because they have to; what if, as leaders, we could provide an
environment that our people actually desired to be a part of?
What if we could create a culture where every teammate wants
to be his best for himself and his teammates?

We want our first case study to help you reflect on the kind
of person who makes most leaders want to trade their chair
for a seat on the next train out of town: underperformers.
Whether now or at some point in our past, we've all shared
the pain that underperformers bring to us as leaders and to
our teams. The funny thing is they obviously didn't start out
that way or chances are they wouldn't be on your team in the
first place. At some point they had to add value, and without a
doubt they had to be engaged in what you're trying to achieve
together. Applying the three commitments reveals what we
need to do for our best people to keep them engaged, for our
folks who might need an extra push to get to the next level,
and for Jack.

You have a Jack in your life, and whether you lead a small team
or a multinational corporation with 1,000 underperformers, he

is driving you crazy. Jack graduated top of his class and came into the interview with an infectious attitude that made you wish you had a cloning device to spread it around to the rest of the team. Obviously, you hired him and expected great things. Jack was on the fast track—a hire you bragged about to your colleagues and talked about at the dinner table with your spouse.

After a few months though, Jack's numbers began to tumble. In addition, he is now often late, and his attitude is dismissive on good days. Was Jack's talent smoke and mirrors? Possibly, although odds are that Jack is lacking something he needs from you. Sure, he controls his own behavior, and maybe you inherited him onto your team. But Jack is still an opportunity. We have talented people on our teams who we know can produce more than they are. When they don't, it is our problem. Too often, at least in part, it's also our fault. Not that we've intentionally done anything wrong. We've told them what we thought and been as good to them as every other teammate. That is often the Achilles' heel of a leader: we try to treat everyone the same.

No one on our team is the same. Each person has a unique way of thinking, working, and interacting. The leaders who we study, admire, and hold up to all generations as people we want to emulate treated everyone on their teams as individuals. Even when they were creating strategy, goals, and game plans, they never lost sight of the impact those endeavors would have on every person's life. They committed to a way of treating people so when they made mistakes, their people still trusted them; together with their team, they were ready for the most difficult moments.

To meet the needs of every individual on our team, we first fulfill the commitments in everyday conversations. Leadership is not just about the big moments on stage, the championship victories, and the biggest of ideas; it's about how we connect in ordinary times that make it possible for us and our teams to succeed when we're in the spotlight. When we recognize that a teammate like Jack is struggling, we schedule two one-on-one conversations on back-to-back days with a primary, simple goal: help Jack find clarity.

Clarity Starts with Two Conversations

We're not about to present a superpowered, one-size-fits-all method to fix every underperformer. However, this is an application of the three commitments that we've used thousands of times in various settings, and this approach (or your variation) can make leadership the kind of experience we want to have over and over—the kind of experience our teammates love to have with us.

If you have a big team, it might feel stressful to try to schedule two meetings with all the people you want to help improve. Again, you don't have to do this overnight. And as leaders, we have to create the personal time with each of our teammates: so they know we value them and because we become better leaders every time we help develop a teammate's potential. To start developing Jack, the first conversation is short, around five to ten minutes, and the second lasts for an hour and should be scheduled for the following day.

In your first meeting, you're ready to set the stage for Jack to become the talented performer you know he can be. But when he walks in the room, you can already see in his eyes that he's expecting a bad conversation. This is the point where most of us fail Jack and unintentionally sabotage our leadership ethos. We're under pressure, and we just want Jack to do what we know he's capable of doing. Instead of truly taking the time to listen, he experiences us as a parent disciplining a child. The stressed-out leader says something like, "Jack, what's wrong with you?"

The leader who is paying attention to Jack, his potential, and the ways we can snap him out of his performance coma says, "You have been on my mind, and I want to reconnect. Jack, I want to get to know you better."

His eyes will pop open. When you say, "I know you've got huge talent; that's why you're on this team, and I want us to figure out together what you need in order to be successful here," he might actually sit up a little straighter. If you can do it authentically, you can go further and say, "I want to figure out how to help you do great things."

Almost sounds too crazy—but not if we want to lead. Our teammates need us to loan them our confidence. They need us to believe in them so they can stop wasting their time wondering if they're good enough and spend all their energy proving to themselves what they can really do. They need to be clear that we believe in them before they will take the risks to do what will be difficult or new.

In almost every case, Jack will be on the edge of his seat thrilled for a chance to make things right. If not, it means things have been going so badly that he doesn't trust you or his personal life is so troubled that he can't keep his chin above water. Whatever the reason, stay focused on the clarity you're trying to help him experience. You can ask, "Do you mind if I ask you a couple of questions to get to know you better?" Asking permission to have a more personal conversation is a critical step that's not traditionally part of work culture, but it's essential. Leaders who want to create clarity can't do it by telling someone what to think. We have to discover what Jack thinks, so we can create understanding in what we work on together.

Next, ask him to think about two questions, but don't have him answer them right away:

1. "What do you want to do?" If you are in a work environment, you might need to add, "What is your long-term career goal?"
2. "Why is that important to you?"

These questions are about getting clear on the person's true desires. Before the end of the meeting, emphasize that you would like to have him spend some time on both questions and that you'll meet again to discuss it. Because you believe in his talent, you need to know what he really wants so you can support him in realizing it.

Giving him the second question explores his true motivation, which will become invaluable in keeping him on track as you work through achieving these goals together. If he tries to answer either question on the spot, ask him to pause and reflect on the questions in the time between the meetings. Most of the time, especially when people know they aren't living up to their potential, they will answer with what they think we want to hear.

Jack either doesn't know the answers or believe his own answers, or he'd be performing better. The key here is that you have a conversation about what Jack wants, not what he thinks you want him to be, regardless of how it ties to his current role. There are no repercussions here if he's being honest, and he needs to know that. Regardless of what he wants to do in life, there will be something that will tie back to what he's doing today. The trick is that you can't help him to make that connection unless he is entirely honest with his replies.

When Jack arrives for your second meeting the next day, he's wearing a tie. He hadn't worn a tie since the interview. You start by saying that you've been looking forward to the follow-up and ask how he's feeling. Jack answers, "I am excited and a little nervous." Some of the people you work with will be able to be this honest. Others will wear a mask, trying to give you the right answers in fear of retribution if their goals don't align with their current role. The dialogue we're about to give is an example of how the conversation can go. Notice the way the leader listens and responds. The goal is not to get the same answers from each person but rather to begin to build a connection where we as leaders can support each teammate as he discovers his answers.

You say, "So tell me, what have you been thinking about since our last meeting?" The question has to be open—meaning it can't be answered with a yes or no—so he has room to express his point of view.

Jack says that he really appreciates having a chance to talk about this with you and has a few thoughts. He says, "I know I can do better. I've always tried to be the best at what I do. I feel like I have been trying, but I don't really know how the business works. I know what I'm capable of and what I'm supposed to do, but I can't see how it all fits together."

Notice the numerous places in this one answer where you can help Jack find clarity. He wants to know:

• How he can improve
• The details of how the business operates

- The strategy and vision that ties the organization together
- Where he can help make the maximum impact

Each person you work with will express different areas where they want clarity. The key here is that if his answers appear to be genuine, then he trusts you. That trust can go a long way toward repairing even the most difficult situations, so you're both already part of the way there. If your teammate doesn't trust you, the first commitment reveals what you need to do: seek clarity. When you both have clarity, you can feel the trust building because there is nothing to hide.

As leaders, we usually like to solve problems or help people figure out what to do next. We like to take action. This is an exercise in analysis and getting to know your teammate, so don't jump into solution-finding mode and begin to take on any of these opportunities yet. That's often what kills trust. First, keep listening and keep building his belief in you; he has to be clear that your top priorities are what's in his best interest and giving him the support he needs. If you problem solve too quickly, you won't help Jack get to a place where he has full insight into what he really wants in a way you can both always refer to. He needs to know that you buy into what he wants to accomplish, not just mandate that it happen.

To keep creating a strong memory of the experience for Jack, the kind of experience he'll thank you for years later, reflect what you hear. Say something like, "That's the kind of energy and enthusiasm I saw the first times I met you. Tell me more." Again, open-ended reflections and questions will keep Jack talking about what's important; as he talks, that's when he feels connected to you.

In some cases, the person will talk for a long time about past successes or things he has always wanted to do with his life. This doesn't mean he is wrong for your organization—for instance, if he wants to open a restaurant and you sell widgets. He is telling you what he really thinks, and what matters most is that you pay serious attention.

When he begins to really show the enthusiasm, say something like, "I can see the passion you have for . . . ," then ask to hear more. Every place you establish clarity—that you have heard him, that you value his thoughts, that you believe in his talent—it becomes a marker in time that he will always be grateful for and a marker in your work together that you can continually refer to in order to help Jack make progress.

When he finishes—not when you finish, but when he pauses and looks up expectantly after just having made himself vulnerable—ask, "What do you need to be successful?"

"I don't know," Jack replies. He doesn't know, and few of us do when put in this situation. Here's your chance to take the lead.

You say, "Jack, I hear a passionate, committed, articulate young man who wants to succeed. Am I right?"

He nods.

You say, "Remember when I asked why this was important to you? This is what truly makes you happy, correct?" He nods again. "What if we could find a way for the work we do to contribute to your happiness?" At this point, you notice that same infectious smile you saw in Jack's face back on the day you first interviewed him. The smile and energy is your cue to move forward.

You say, "Jack, here is what I think we do next." Now you can dive into the places you've heard where you can help him gain deeper clarity. Simply because you took the time to listen and get to know him better, he will now be ready to become the success you both want him to be.

This isn't the only way to have this kind of conversation. Throughout this book, we're not telling you exactly what to do; rather, we're exploring *why* fulfilling the three commitments matters to you and your people. The examples and exercises we provide have worked in other settings, and they will either work for you or suggest a method that you can adapt to your situation.

The first two conversations with Jack illustrate the importance of seeking clarity. When it's not a crisis situation, such as when Kennedy and his men were in the water, our first job is to listen. We want to truly understand what Jack wants to do; if we assume we know the answer from a few sentences, he will feel that we really don't want to hear what he has to say. After listening, when we can feel his engagement, we can deliver our message with clarity: that we believe in him and we want to provide him with whatever he needs to be the rock star we know he can be. Jack's new clarity provides the awareness he needs to be successful, but it won't translate into results unless he has stability.

The First Move Towards Stability

Awareness is the first step, but until Jack's behavior changes, he can't produce the results he needs in any environment to have the life he wants—and we simply won't enjoy working with him. Changing his experience and ours is about giving Jack the support he needs in order to feel confident enough to make a transformation. The second commitment we make as leaders: provide and help people find stability. The important next step, one of the fundamental ways to provide stability, is creating a development plan. We will give you a catalog of additional possibilities in the chapter on stability, but this is one of the first steps we have to take with every teammate.

You don't run a marathon without a training schedule. As a musician, you don't go on stage without a tuner, a bottle of water, and at least the first few songs of your set list. But remember, it's not *our* plan for Jack; it's his plan that we help him create. Our role, the way we commit to creating stability for him, is to make sure he has a plan; as with all three commitments, the real value is to make sure Jack owns his ability to foster stability in his own work and life.

If you're already familiar with development plans, you may be thinking this is a management tool. Too often, planning can be a management exercise because it's something we are forced to do once or twice a year because we are people who hold the title of manager. When it is done proactively and becomes a part of how we develop our people, it can also become the kind of experience we need to focus on as leaders.

The vision we provide to people is not just one of what we can do together as a team or in our organization, but it's also one in which we see what each teammate is capable of. It's the vision that differentiates management from leadership. Most of us need to be led to those first steps where we fulfill our potential. The development plan exercise is the intentional act of leading a teammate to his future self: the person he really wants to be and you need him to be.

In your next conversation, to create the right plan for him you ask:

- What are the most important tasks for you to do?
- What will you need (resources, support, opportunities) to be successful?
- How will we measure your efforts and results?

Usually you want to give the person these questions before this meeting. You want to have answers as well, as most of our people will stumble when planning in this manner. It's hard, both because he may have never done this kind of planning and he knows this is serious. When a teammate struggles, we have to provide stability so he can overcome the inertia of his fear or doubt.

Most of us have never created a true development plan before. A lot of our plans are pushed down from the top: our leaders tell us what to do, and we're expected to fall in line. Of course, there will be things the organization needs from Jack, but this is his personal development plan, so he can be of maximum value to himself and the organization. He owns and drives it; we create the environment for him to practice and ultimately succeed. When you're finished with that conversation, create a list:

- **What** he's working on
- The **help** you need to provide him, so he can hold you accountable
- The **measurements** you'll both use to track his progress

Not only does the plan generate clarity and agreement about the steps of making the work we do together productive, we've proved as a leader that we're committed to him.

Having this kind of conversation is not just for leading at work. When we're coaching, it's how we show teammates that we care about their progress. As a leader in a community, whether we apply this to a one-on-one relationship, a committee, or a movement, the information we discover together connects us to a person for life. When we ask people about what they want, how it can happen through your work together, and then the plan to make that work flourish, they'll never forget the attention and they'll always remember the way we led.

The Best Kind of Meetings

Most of the time, when we spend time fulfilling the commitments with our people, they'll start trying to fulfill the commitments for themselves. The first three meetings create the clarity and stability we need to want to work together. To deepen the insight and strengthen the trust, however, the kind of conversations we had with Jack initially must become a repeatable pattern.

Regular meetings, whether formal or informal, monitor the progress and determine if adjustments to the plan are required: either what Jack's doing, how we support him, or how we measure the results. Just as on a GPS in our cars, to get from one place to another we have to know where we are and where we want to go. When we're clear and we have stability, we're ready to move toward what we want.

The fourth sit-down is to figure out the regular meetings and ways you'll work together. While the first two commitments provide the insight and behaviors a teammate needs to achieve the life he wants, if he can't repeat them or if the repetition doesn't happen with an ease that makes what he has to do habitual, he still doesn't have the environment he needs.

The final commitment is to create a rhythm so natural that whatever the person has to do becomes a daily and weekly pattern—a pattern so fluid that it happens with minimal fear or worry. After a few weeks, Jack's numbers are already better. But he comes into your office, and even though you're happy, he's not. "I know I can do more," he says. You may not be used to this kind of enthusiasm.

Teammates want more when they experience a leader who commits to creating an environment where they can be successful. The easiest way to create rhythm for every team-mate is a regular review of how things have been progressing, both positively and the things that need to improve, based on regular measurement. Most people are afraid of being judged. They don't want to know the numbers that go along with how they are performing. Usually, that's because they don't have the clarity about what they're doing or the stability from which to act. Measurement can also shut teammates down when it's not part of the regular rhythm of working together.

In this case, you decide to have lunch with Jack once a week. That's how easy it can be. (If you're leading a team of 40, weekly meetings are impossible, but regular conversations are still essential.) It's not a formal review, just a back-and-forth about how Jack feels about his progress and the places he gets stuck. You review the numbers and use that as a springboard into a conversation about how he's doing. Then, at the end of each conversation, you reaffirm the plan (clarity), which also reestablishes your commitment to support him in the way he needs you (stability), and confirms the measurement you'll use again at your next meeting as together you tweak the patterns of his work to a place where he truly loves what he's doing (rhythm).

Again, an immediate critique of these meetings is that this is not leadership—it's mentoring or management. Yes. Both disciplines are necessary, even for the leader; they are in fact tools of leadership. What qualifies these interactions with your teammates as leadership is that you're committing to their talent. You're not only reflecting and trying to bring the person along as a mentor; you also have a vision as leader that you need them to help you achieve. You're not only checking on results, which is the function of the manager, but you're also tying those results to why what you're doing together matters. Leadership uses the skills of mentoring and management to maximize the impact, trust, and production of our work as a team, and ties it to the greater purposes we're fighting for together.

What Kind of Leader Do You Want to Be?

It doesn't matter where you are in your development as a leader. What matters is how you lead today.

Some people may say Kennedy was a failed leader because his ship sunk. In fact his brother Joe sent him a letter after reading about the incident: "What I really want to know," he wrote, "is where the hell were you when the destroyer hove into sight, and exactly what were your moves?" We know Kennedy cried over the two men who died in the accident and then started leading again. He inspired a world of leaders through the leadership actions of a lifetime. Like Kennedy continuing to fight in the war, and ultimately becoming president, even though we make mistakes, we can all use the three commitments to lead our people to new realities.

This is like when we work with the other Jacks in our lives. No one on our team wants to underperform. No human being just wants to sit in his cubicle and collect a paycheck.

As leaders, it is our role to help him find the place where he wants to and can make an impact. It is our job to be the kind of leader who believes in him even when he doesn't believe in himself. It is our job to make the three commitments, to create the kind of environment where every person on our team can be the kind of leader we want to be: worthy of trust and capable of producing extraordinary results.

CHAPTER 2

CLARITY

What Is the Commitment to Clarity?

The first commitment is clarity. The quest for clarity is an ancient problem. Whether we like it or not, our communication and action does not always send the message we intend or produce the effect we hope for. The Greeks personified the human problem with clarity in Eris, the goddess of confusion. Wherever she went, trouble followed. The ancient Greeks' most-told story about the kind of trouble a lack of clarity can perpetrate occurred when Eris was not invited to the wedding of Achilles' parents. As the rest of Olympus reveled, she tossed a golden apple into the party with the inscription *Kallisiti*, "for the most beautiful one."

Just like in our teams and organizations, when we don't know our goals, roles, and reasons for what we're achieving together, chaos ensues. All Eris had to do was throw an apple with a few words on it and the other goddesses began quarrelling about who was the fairest. The initial lack of clarity allowed Zeus to select Paris, the prince of Troy, to choose the fairest of them all. What happened next? Bribes for Paris from the goddesses desperate to be the fairest, which included Aphrodite's offer of the legendary beauty Helen, wife of the Spartan king Menelaus. Paris, man that he was, chose Helen, not seeing clearly the trouble he was about to cause—and the Trojan War began. From a simple apple and a cryptic phrase, Troy was destroyed.

When confusion enters the places where we lead, it can very easily lead down a path to destruction. As leaders, we may be quickly distracted, creating battles inside ourselves and among our teams that could be avoided with a little clarity about the ends that will result from our choices and the real problems we're trying to solve. Clarity is the first commitment because too often we act without enough of it. We make choices and take action without enough reflection about where we're really going and why. Then people follow us, and they turn into grumpy bears because they didn't know what we were getting them into.

We never reach a state of perfect clarity. The U.S. Army has changed its definition of leadership at least 14 times since 1948. Does that mean that the organization that produces more leaders than any other on earth is unclear about what leadership is? Just the opposite: it exhibits that our world is always changing, and as our situations change, what it means to lead changes. What doesn't change is the fundamental environment everyone requires to be successful: we need transparent awareness about every critical piece of information that affects what we're trying to do. We need deep understanding in us and in every person on our team so confusion doesn't throw an apple of discord into the important work we're accomplishing together.

As leaders we can try to be clear in every speech, meeting, e-mail, and delegation. We must *seek to understand* what's going on in the lives of our people and our cultures, and match our leadership to the minds of those whom we serve. Old-school leadership was about the people aligning with the leader; in our world today, we are all capable and need to lead in a deeply global, interconnected planet, and so it is everyone's responsibility to align with one another.

First, the commitment to clarity is the dedication to constantly foster an awareness of everything that needs to be known for each member of a team to be successful. And second, in addition to clear instructions, the commitment is about seeking to be clear in each interaction. It is about creating a mind-set that together we will explore everything which needs to be known so thoroughly that we both understand what we're doing, how to do it best, and why the actions we take together will produce the results we both want.

Beginning with clarity, here's the most important point that differentiates the three commitments from other approaches to leadership: it is a model of interaction that leaders and teammates do together. We can't produce clarity by telling people what they need to know. We can't force clarity into the mind of another person. The awareness happens as we seek the answers together.

The commitment to clarity is about making sure there is commonality of understanding. No one finds clarity in the same way. Our past experiences, our burdens and joys, and people we've learned from set us up to discover new insights; it is the leader's privilege to understand the way each teammate receives information. That doesn't mean in times of crisis, such as when JFK was with his men in the water, we don't give orders. It means that long before we ever have moments in which we need to give orders, we've built connections that allow us to survive and ultimately thrive through any crisis.

We can lead by telling people what to do, and it may even create clarity about the tasks they need to accomplish. What it won't do is create an environment where what is produced takes advantage of the unique insight and capabilities each of us has to offer.

Blind Men Baking Bread

Leadership experiment Number Two: how would you help a team of blind men bake bread?

What would you do first? Most of us would doubt the project is even possible. We'd think, "Really? Blind men and ovens? That's about as safe as bringing a grizzly bear to teach preschool." They could get burned, set the kitchen on fire, or worse, have to eat bad bread.

Each leadership experiment is about centering our minds on what we do *first* and how we can be most valuable to our teams and organizations. Where the sinking ship experiment was about the grounding of all leadership and bringing others along with you, this clarity experiment is about what's possible for us as leaders when we get clear and when we help others get clear about what we can do together.

Think about the blind men again. Who are they? They've probably spent their entire lives hearing about what they can't do. Think about all the places where others have to take care of them. Why would they want to bake bread? What if they want to do something for their friends or family? What if the fighter in each of them also wants to bake bread because it's something that the world thinks a blind man can't do?

What would you do first?

Did you want to start by figuring out how they will bake in spite of their handicap? That's not wrong, but when things start getting messy—and with a team of blind men, they will—what will keep you wanting to work together? Did you want to immediately come up with a plan? Also a great response, but as leaders, if we plan before we know why what we're doing really matters, how do we help our team stay on course when they don't like the plan or want to stick to it?

Did you answer "Figure out why they want to bake bread"? Like with Jack, we cannot help people accomplish anything—from being valuable members of our team to discovering that they can lead too—if we don't understand what motivates and moves them. Working with the blind men could be an unbelievably satisfying experience, a story you'd tell for the rest of your life. But like on most teams, if we don't know our people, we can't adjust our leadership to help them be their best and achieve what we know they can accomplish.

Clarity is not something that can be dictated or given, it is created when we explore what we're trying to do and why, so that each person with whom we work knows what her role is, and we know how to talk about her work in a way that makes sense to her. The experiment with the blind men is about how you regard people. Is a member of your team just someone you use to get things done—a tool who needs to do his assignment like a robot; or is he a partner and potentially a fellow leader whom you can connect with? All the members of our teams are blind until they have clarity.

Do You Have Clarity?

The starting point of fulfilling any commitment is ourselves as leaders. To build a team or an organization in which the culture is something people want to be a part of, we have to be able to live the commitments for ourselves before we can ever have a true impact on the environment or others.

Clarity begins with the consciousness of what we know and what we don't know. It is the simplest of realities, and the reason it is the first commitment as a leader is because it is the most dangerous thing when it is missing. When we're confused, we can't act. When a leader is unclear, a team is left guessing. There are probably hundreds, if not thousands, of things you have to be clear about in the places you lead. We're not going to dig into every single one. The commitment model does that on its own. Hold clarity as a lens to any situation and you know if you or your people have it or not. And there are specific areas of our lives as leaders where we believe every leader needs to be clear in order to be the kind of person people want to follow. Ask yourself three questions:

1. **What do I want?** We often think leaders are supposed to lead for noble reasons. Yes, and we think our reasons, the desires of our life, are the noblest purposes we can work for. We won't be fired up for long if what we're doing is someone else's cause; it has to be our purpose too. If we haven't been honest about what we want, how can anyone on our team be honest either? What we want always shows up—either in our unhappiness because we're not getting it or working toward it, or in our infectious enthusiasm for what we're doing. If the question isn't enough, we'll provide an exercise further on to help you and your teammates get clear about what you really want from them, and we'll explore the story of a leader who used the clarity of her deep desire to save hundreds of lives.

2. **Why is the place where I'm leading important?** The cause is not enough, but the cause still matters. Even if we're working in a business or organization almost by accident—by circumstances rather than by planning—within the purpose of an organization are reasons that we can own. Even if you don't love the place you work or what you're working on, there are still aspects of the experience you can invest yourself in—and you have to. Leaders can always find important work to do wherever they are.

3. **Why do I lead?** It doesn't matter how powerful our storytelling is or how compelling the case studies about organizations that fulfill the three commitments will be—if you don't know why you lead, you'll stop. You'll have to stop because you're going to face challenges, moments, or possibly years where what to do next isn't entirely clear, and knowing why you lead is the fuel to keep going.

We commit to clarity as leaders because if we're not motivated to push through the unexpected challenges—the days when people just can't do what they need to do—it is better not to lead. It is better to leave a leadership position empty or fill it with an interim leader than step into the responsibility without the motivation to keep going until we complete the mission we signed up for. With clarity about what you want, the value of the place you lead, and why you are a leader, you'll not only be unstoppable in your life, your clarity will be absorbed by the people around you. They will commit to clarity because you did, and keep leading when you can't. As you'll discover in our next story, clear leaders can help their teammates reach goals they thought would never happen.

Dead Men Tell No Tales

When we commit to clarity, the people around us can do the things that scare them the most and achieve results they never imagined. Leadership is about getting connected to the people we serve so we understand their struggles and desires. It demands that we push ourselves and those we work with in ways that help them sort out the uncertainty that creates confusion. That pushing can have an edge, and it needs to when everything is at stake.

Harriet Tubman may be one of the bravest human beings in history. If saving a life is priceless, as a leader, she is also one of the most undervalued. Her life began as a slave, but her life as a leader began on September 17, 1849, when she escaped from a Maryland plantation with her brothers. As they left, knowing what she wanted, she sang "I'll meet you in the morning, I'm bound for the Promised Land." But the trip became more dangerous from the start. Her brothers, afraid they would be recaptured, even in the free North, changed their minds. They chose slavery over their sister and went back to their shackled lives.

Tubman, without money or safe passage, like so many seeking freedom, followed the North Star to the hiding places and homes on the Underground Railroad. When we try to do more—more than others can imagine, more than we've done before, even more than the world has ever seen—we are thrust into the lead. We don't know how that experience is going to change us. When Tubman arrived in Philadelphia, the moment she was free she realized she had to go back to Maryland. She said in her biography,

I knew a man who was sent to the State Prison for twenty-five years. All these years he was always thinking of his home, and counting by years, months, and days, the time till he should be free, and see his family and friends once more. The years roll on, the time of imprisonment is over, and the man is free. He leaves the prison gates, he makes his way to his old home, but his old home is not there. The house in which he had dwelt in his childhood had been torn down, and a new one had been put up in its place; his family were gone, their very name was forgotten, there was no one to take him by the hand to welcome him back to his life.

So it was with me. I had crossed the line of which I had so long been dreaming. I was free; but there was no one to welcome me to the land of freedom. I was a stranger in a strange land, and my home after all was down in the old cabin quarter, with the old folks, and my brothers and sisters. But to this solemn resolution I came; I was free and they should be free also. . . .

She started with her niece and her children, then her brother and two other men. Her first return trip was in the spring of 1850. Ignoring the fugitive slave law that required Northern authorities to return runaways, she took people all the way to Canada. She went south 19 more times, often with a $40,000 bounty on her head (over $1 million today). Estimates differ, but Tubman was personally responsible for freeing another 70 to 300 slaves through the Underground Railroad.

The story of Harriet Tubman and her resolve is famous. What has often been overlooked is what made her so powerful as a leader. Not only did she know what she wanted, but she realized why: "That [her people] should be free also." Moreover, she applied ingenious methods of creating clarity for others: conductors like Tubman, the leaders who brought the slaves through a series of homes and secret shelters provided by abolitionist men and women fighting against the institution of slavery, had a quiver of techniques to make the trip to safety possible.

The first was song. There has never been a clearer common language than the spirituals used by slaves to communicate right under the noses of the owners who wanted to keep them in chains. Two of the common forms, signal songs and map songs, gave instructions that only those seeking freedom would understand. Signal songs told others of an event, like when it was time to leave. For example, the day Tubman left for the first time, she sang, "I'll meet you in the morning, I'm bound for the Promised Land." Map songs, such as "Follow the Drinking Gourd," kept those seeking freedom walking under the North Star. In both cases, secret communication translated only to those who needed it and yet clearly transmitted the intended message.

The second technique was a set of behaviors that kept the men and women seeking freedom safe. When Tubman reached homes, she showed her fellow passengers exactly what they needed to do to avoid the authorities: blend in. Playing on the expectations of the Southern mind, the fleeing slaves acted as if they were servants in the homes of the families that were actually setting them free. On her first trip, she swept the yard. On another, she put on a bonnet and carried chickens to appear like she was running errands. Because many people assumed all black people were illiterate, Tubman could always pick up a newspaper and hide in plain sight. She didn't have time to teach people complicated deceptions, so everything she did was something they could do instantly. Fulfilling the commitment to clarity means we find ways to make clear what our people need to do to be successful, and we do it in a way that fits the environment in which we lead.

Her third method won't work in the corporate world, but it is the kind of direct persuasion leaders have to use sometimes in the most treacherous situations. There was no limit to what Tubman was willing to do to protect the freedom of her passengers: she carried a revolver. She had a famous line that immediately let those with her overcome their fear when they wanted to turn back. When the people she was helping had wearied, with bloody feet and guts full of doubt and somehow thinking slavery was better than what lay ahead, Tubman would put her gun to their heads and threaten, "Dead [men] tell no tales. You go on, or die." Once we're clear as leaders about our goals, roles, and reasons, we foster an environment that helps our teammates stay clear—it's not always easy, and sometimes it takes extremely creative or direct methods.

With the clarity she created through song, easily teachable methods of avoiding capture, and her willingness to help people make the hard choices no matter what, she helped hundreds discover clarity about what their lives could become and actually reach freedom. Her journeys not only inspired every family on the Underground Railroad to keep working for the cause, but prominent leaders of the day. Abolitionists such as Frederick Douglass, and politicians like Lincoln's Secretary of State, William Seward, were strengthened by her courage in their own fight for the cause of universal freedom. Her story became the bane of Southern slave owners, the hope of every bonded man and woman, and the inspiration for tens of thousands of abolitionists wanting to see the institution ended.

Add, Keep, Delete

In situations like the one with Kennedy in the water with his men or when Tubman was on the road with people seeking freedom, those leaders fulfilled the commitments by instinct. But as leaders, we have to tune our instincts with preparation. Leaders, who are ready in crisis, have done the kind of exercises and reflection we'll suggest in the chapters on each commitment. These are not the only ways to create clarity, stability, and rhythm; they are the ways we've discovered or found that other successful leaders and organizations have used to create environments for teams to fulfill the commitments.

As it will be with each commitment, finding clarity is personal, whether for you or as you help a teammate. How many mandates have you followed and felt empowered afterward? When everyone—from your parents to your first coaches, teachers, and bosses—told you what to do, did you like it? Now remember the person who helped you discover what you wanted to do. Think about the times you've made intentional choices to do what mattered most to you. That's what we can, as leaders, do everyday for our people and for ourselves.

Add, keep, delete—like going through your closet of clothes or your tools in the garage and deciding what you want to keep, save, or give away—is a method of creating an inventory of the things we truly value in our lives. Many of us stress over what we don't have, but we never take the time to truly define what is missing. Start by making a list in three columns:

- **Column 1.** If you could add anything you wanted to your life, anything at all, what would you add?

Then ask and insert a second column to your list.

- **Column 2.** What are the things in your life you want to keep? In the pursuit of what you want to add, what are you going to try and keep no matter what?

Finally ask, and create a third column.

- **Column 3.** In the pursuit of what you want and the
  effort to keep what is most important to you, what are
  you willing to get rid of or let go of?

We often chase after things we *think* we want. Outside
stimuli—bosses and family, cultural products such as com-
mercials and films, and environmental influences like where
we work and the habits of neighbors and friends—pull us to be
like them or fulfill their visions for our lives. In the pursuit of
things we actually never really wanted, we may risk the things
we value most and the precious parts of our life we want to
keep. As leaders, we have to constantly pay attention to where
we're going, or we may end up in the wrong place.

By focusing on the adds and keeps, we gain clarity that lets
us make quicker and better choices about opportunities and
challenges. Having this focus also lets us reassess our prior
choices. Do the things we do and have still meet our needs?
If not, we can get rid of them and create space in our lives for
what helps us get more of what we want and retain more of
what we value.

You can do this exercise daily for yourself. When you know
what you want and what you desire to continue doing, as well
as what you want to remove from your life, you have your priorities and your action plan for your day; and a way of measuring if you're making progress toward the life you want.

You can do the same thing with the people you lead. Ask
them what they want to add, keep, and delete, and then help
them figure out how to get what they want and remove the
distractions or burdens. They will leave the conversation with
excitement because they have control over their focus. The

result: both you and your team know what you want and the weight that's been dragging you down that you'll get rid of; each time you repeat the exercise, you'll discover clarity about where to pour your energy.

We Think We've Been Clear

Too many of our teammates aren't excited to work with us because they don't have clarity. We think when we've said something once or sent instructions, our teams will understand and execute our instructions. Ask 10 leaders whom you know whether they give clear instructions to their teams. All will enthusiastically respond, "Of course!"—at least at first. In our heads, we are always clear. That's why we're leaders.

Where we all get stuck sometimes is translating what's in our heads so our teammates are just as clear. We lead because we know what needs to get done and we're ready for action, often when others don't know what to do. Sometimes we need to tell them what to do because otherwise they don't do it. We communicate well; that can be one of the key reasons why we've risen as leaders. When things don't go well, however, we often believe it's because other people weren't listening or didn't receive the e-mail. That is completely understandable; it's an appropriate first feeling.

If you're the CEO of a Fortune 500 corporation, you can absolutely insist on your staff following your instructions. You can tell people how to bring you information, and they will. In fact, it can be the best way to deal with the incredible complexity of the work in a more efficient manner, and in a way that maximizes clear, valuable interactions with the most teammates. If you're in a hierarchical culture like the military, you must demand that subordinates do what you say. When the bullets are flying, direct orders from experienced leaders need to be followed to the letter by every member of the team to do everything possible to keep everyone alive and achieve the objective.

But we can't stop there, not if we are truly leading. When we're working with our closest teammates, our team of leaders, and those we hope will become leaders too, we have to behave differently. When we're with our fellow executives at dinner or with our squad after the battle, the kind of awareness we need to develop is more personal. We have to understand how they think and feel, what makes them want to be on a team, and, ultimately, we have to be clear about what they want in life. The information matters because we can't create an environment where someone will have an impact unless we know the kind of impact they want to have.

If you know that members of your executive team really want to become CEOs, you give them chances to get clear about why, so they can have the experiences with you that will mentor them into the kind of person who can be your successor. For people who are happy staying in finance or HR, you'll still include them in every critical conversation and decision, but your interaction will focus on what they want and care about most. At war, you're not going to give a private who just wants to get home safely the risky job that puts others in danger when another member of the team wants to be a military lifer. Putting the wrong people in circumstances where they're not motivated is dangerous, and that kind of leadership is possible only when we do more than paint the vision, give instructions, and move on.

Paying attention to whether we've been clear is how we create an environment where the group experience makes us all want to keep working for the necessary results. When failure is not an option, as when Tubman kept her passengers safe or when a company has to do enough business to stay solvent, clarity is first the key to survival and the ultimate way to success we dream about. When we think we've been clear with our team and we haven't been, their brains and bodies shut down.

The Sponge and Shortcuts

The biggest obstacle to clarity is also our greatest resource. When is the last time you thought about your brain? What about how your work environment affects your brain or each teammate's brain? Do you craft every interaction, every communication so it's most likely to be understood in the mind of each teammate? Most of us don't, until we realize that the three pounds of gray matter inside our cranium is the linchpin for an environment where people achieve and want to work together.

The information and experiences that make up the environments in which we lead become the content from which every person on our team learns and acts. Whether we can hear what's being said or we're distracted, whether we absorb information or it falls out the other ear, whether we can use what we've heard to formulate great thoughts or the knowledge goes into our unconscious all depends how our brains function in the environment.

We're not psychologists, but the metaphors we'll introduce about the brain in each of the next three chapters are essential knowledge for every leader. The brain's 100 billion neurons fire, sometimes without conscious thought—without effort, like the heart's beating—and other times with intention, like choosing to eat a sandwich rather than a pile of dirt. If you don't know how the brain works in a way you can remember, you can't connect with your people in a way that builds the awareness (clarity), behaviors (stability), and patterns (rhythm) each of us needs to produce the results we hope for. In fact, you may be working in a way that makes it impossible for your people to contribute.

Our brains create chemical reactions based on the environment and situations we are in. These reactions manifest through our mouths as words and with our bodies as the actions we take, creating our personality that other people notice. We've intentionally developed the three commitments to drive us to pay attention to both our brains and the environmental factors that feed them, two aspects of individual and organizational success that too few of us may have even realized were important.

Our brains respond to the environment in two ways: as human beings, first we constantly perceive the world around us, and then we use that information to conceive ideas and responses.

The perceiving brain is a *sponge*: it stores every word, image, and experience. When you listen to a lecture, its phrases and ideas, the response of the crowd, and the style of the speaker all get absorbed into your memory. You may still remember a lecture where the person next to you was attractive and you didn't pay attention to a word the speaker said, you just don't remember the content of the talk. Every time we sit down with a colleague, we store that experience. Every e-mail we send is recorded into the memory, consciously or unconsciously. What we say, our body language, what we look like: our brains keep a record of every interaction and experience filed away for the rest of our lives.

The brain is also like a *laboratory*, where the act of conceiving takes place. Every piece of information that our five senses capture will become the fodder for our mind's immense capacity to process. Every brain can dream and imagine. Waking and sleeping, the brain is taking the data stored and manipulating it. The new science of memory, in fact, has revealed that memories change over time. While the ideas are still being developed, the very act of remembering can change the content of other memories. Our brains are always working on what is stored in our minds, processing what's been experienced in order to fulfill our biological imperative to survive.

Here's where the sponge and the laboratory come together, and why it matters to us as leaders. Give your people information and experiences that are flawed, and what their brain can produce will be defective. Innocuous experiences become evidence that everything is awful. Don't pay attention to what they think and feel—the environment they need to be their best—and they will remember that you didn't notice. And the risk of not being clear is bigger than that.

The brain produces shortcuts. In psychological study, heuristics are the rules of thumb that our brain generates from past experience to solve existing problems. They are the go-to solutions we use to save time and deal with complex situations. Here's an exaggerated example. Our ancient ancestors had to contend with threats we don't face today, such as giant man-eating birds. If our ancient ancestors' eyes perceived a moving shadow, their mind instructed them to run; when they had previously seen a shadow moving, multiple friends had suddenly been plucked up into the air by a fowl of ghastly size. Their brains created a shortcut to get them through the day, even if occasionally they started running from a cloud passing in front of the sun.

The brain produces shortcuts, but they are not always appropriate. If we run from every shadow, we're constantly moving, with all the stress that causes, for no reason. The same thing happens on teams when we're unclear as leaders. If we send mixed messages about core content or the behaviors we need, the wrong shortcuts get built. Some shortcuts are good because they skip steps and allow people to work faster. But heuristics can be bad if they cause people to make decisions based on erroneous information.

Profiling is an example of heuristics. The perfect candidate for a computer programming position, at least on paper and from a few references you checked, shows up to the interview in flip-flops. In the past, you've seen a correlation between the way a person dresses and his talent, so you don't hire the person. Your shortcut is: the way you dress is a sign of talent. The shortcut can obviously work as it reveals a person's level of preparation, for instance, whether he bothered to find out about your office culture. But that shortcut could also backfire, for instance, when your competitor doesn't use it and hires the candidate, and he creates the next YouTube.

Mantras are another form of shortcut. If a team wastes time in long meetings, many of which need to be repeated because key contributors aren't present, a strong leader can suggest a short rule of thumb to determine which meetings should happen and which should be canceled. You suggest that every meeting should have the necessary people in attendance. "The right people at the table" becomes the go-to mantra for how you work together. Your team starts putting meetings together with that mantra in mind, and information no longer has to be repeated at numerous meetings—and pointless meetings no longer happen, because the key players are always there.

The brain's creation of shortcuts is not good or bad; we simply need to be aware of how the sponge between our ears processes everything it experiences. Leaders have the potential, in everything we do, to create the environment in which the necessary information and experience surrounds every teammate and in which the shortcuts that are built promote decision-making that moves toward our shared goals. On the other hand, if we come to work grumpy—when people know the days when we don't smile, they will get yelled at—they'll flee. Their rule of thumb will be to avoid you on your grumpy days. But what if on one of those grumpy days they don't include you in a critical conversation? When we speak, act, and lead poorly, their brains will generate ineffective, potentially disastrous shortcuts.

This doesn't mean we always have to be smiling when we lead. It means we always have to pay attention to how what we do provides information our teams use to create clarity. We simply can't forget that the whole time their brains are like a sponge, soaking up the culture around them. At the same time, like a laboratory running experiments, their memory is being formed and reformed, creating shortcuts that will either hinder or accelerate your progress.

Asking Why

A powerful shortcut and another exercise you can use whenever clarity eludes you or a teammate is the question "why?" As add-keep-delete helps us get clear on what we want, the question "why?" used over and over digs deep into the reasons that ultimately drive our actions. "The Five Whys" was originally created by the Toyota Motor Corporation as a process improvement tool, but the method is also an exquisite way to create clarity with individuals or teams. The purpose of this exercise is to use a very simple question to determine the root cause of any issue that's causing confusion. Sometimes it is about what you're doing; other times your question is about understanding why what you're doing matters.

We've used the question "why?" since we learned to speak. As children, we needed to understand everything about the environment around us to satisfy our curious brains, and it was cute until the seventh time it was asked. But as adults, the question is essential. It's about discovering our answers beyond what we think we're supposed to say and do. It's about focusing our memory on what really matters. This exercise can be difficult at first, but the outcome can save you and your team hours, possibly days, of reworking and missed deadlines going forward.

Here's how it plays out. Start with the issue that needs more clarity, and simply ask yourself "why?" or construct a question that starts with *why*. Be honest, brutally honest. Most of us can answer the first one or two layers of "why?" While you may be tempted to jump into finding solutions, don't. Not yet. Take your first answer and again ask "why?" If the answer is a challenge, you're getting there. If it's still a fairly easy exercise, rinse and repeat, and it's very likely that it soon won't be.

For instance, if your problem is, "I didn't hit my metrics or goal according to our performance management system," here is how "The Five Whys" could play out.

- **Why?** Because I didn't understand how the system worked.
- **Why?** Because I wasn't trained on the new process.

- **Why?** Because I didn't ask for help.
- **Why?** Because I was afraid to appear incompetent.
- **Why?** Because my boss has a habit of firing people he thinks can't do the job.

Does the example above look familiar? The problem statement and first two layers have been recited countless times, and as leaders we typically stop there and jump into the solution of training everyone on our teams on the "how" of their job all over again.

But that's often not the real issue. The root of the issue in this case is why the person couldn't or didn't fulfill the how of her role. Until the why is addressed, this individual and ultimately your team will never perform at the level you need; it's when she can always tell you why she is always clear about how to have maximum impact on whatever you're doing together. Sometimes people can't answer the question "why?" because our organizations, or we as the leaders in charge of making the big decisions, haven't been clear about the core knowledge every teammate needs. In every case, the question "why" becomes a secret weapon and the go-to solution for generating a deep, memorable clarity.

Puzzle Pieces

Another reason clarity is the first commitment: the amount of information flooding every human being's brain is not going to slow down, and this is the case in every organization, community, and country. The number of things—messages, personal needs, people, business demands—that require our attention is like a puzzle with 20,000 pieces that has just been dumped on our desk, and most of the time we don't know where to start.

Our case studies and exercises so far have been about individual leaders paying attention to clarity. In organizations, we have to pay just as much attention to creating an environment where everything a teammate soaks up gives him the opportunity to be clear about how he can have an impact on the work we're trying to accomplish in his own way. Give directions and expect them to be followed: that's treating someone like a cog. If we commit to clarity, we open up the opportunity for each person to have an influence in ways that we might never have imagined.

There is a wide range of places in which we need clarity on a team or in an organization. Sometimes it's the larger vision of where we're going; sometimes it's a specific deadline or requirement that defines what we do. Regardless of what kind of clarity we need, the commitment to it is about helping teammates take in the information they need so the shortcuts focus them directly on what they can do to have an impact on the overall process. None of us feel valuable unless we know where we fit and why what we do matters.

No matter where you lead, there are a handful of places where everyone needs clarity. These are the first puzzle pieces that allow a team to connect with one another and start moving together. Look at companies or groups that are achieving; all members either have the information they need to be successful or they know where they can get it. We're about to break down some of the core places in which we've seen the best organizations create clarity with their people.

We're intentionally using companies you know well. They've been written about a lot, and that's the point: they've achieved a way of thinking and operating that is very transparent—looking in from the outside, all of us have clarity about what the leaders do to create an environment where the team succeeds. This list is not complete or the ultimate catalog of where you need to be clear; it's a starting point. The places you need to create clarity depend on your specific field. And, in every field, if you're not as clear as the leaders of these teams in these areas, you know where you need to start.

Whom Do You Serve?

Who is your customer? Sometimes it is your end consumer, and other times it includes your internal partners. Sometimes it is teammates in another department who depend upon your work, or a business partner with whom you're collaborating. Most of us serve many people in what we do, but in every case we need to define whom our work is for and what they need from us. Obvious? Yes. But can you as a leader describe whom you serve in a sentence? Can every person on your team? Do the answers of every person on your team align?

Trader Joe's is one of the fastest growing retail brands in America. Although it began as a convenience store in 1967, it quickly became home for Southern California food and beverage shoppers with adventurous taste. TJ's knows its customers: they are educated, looking for value in international products served up in a completely unique shopping experience with the intimate feel of a historic mom-and-pop grocery store. TJ's has kept every store consistent in character from the original 17 sites in the 1970s to the over 270 stores today.

The chain knows the kind of people it needs as well. While producing triple the revenues per square foot than a traditional grocery store, TJ's has created a culture on each team where every teammate has the personality to serve her core shopper, and the training she needs to completely satisfy the store's core demographic. Employees are hired for their enthusiasm and energy. They're asked to leave after 30 days if they're not having fun. Every employee receives training that includes communication, leadership, and teamwork, in addition to a complete understanding of every product. The clearest example of the depth TJ's goes to take care of customers: every employee taste tests every product.

And the training and product knowledge informs the customer experience in the store. If you drop a bottle of wine in Trader Joe's and it smashes all over the ground, multiple employees will come to clean it up, apologize for the inconvenience, have another crew member grab you another bottle, and thank you for your patience as they clean up the mess. Every crew member is trained to do each of the jobs in the store, so every employee is ready to take care of you when you need it—or leave you alone to explore the new tastes they've added that week.

What Need Do You Satisfy?

The need you take care of for your customer—whether you're in manufacturing, professional services, or technology; whether you make sure the recycling is picked up throughout your town, or you're training everyone in your organization in effective presentation—has to be obvious for each teammate. We can't just tell them what to do; we have to create a culture where understanding what we do together is a constant revelatory experience. Each time we satisfy the need that we've come together as a team to serve or solve, it reinforces the value of what we do together.

One of the early twenty-first-century examples of a need perfectly satisfied is actually based on a need the world never knew it had: Zappos. The online store sells shoes—and clothes, bags, and other accessories. The world did not need another shoe store. What the world didn't know it needed was a buying experience, entirely from home, that made purchasing shoes as pleasurable as showing off those new Manolos or old-school Nikes.

Zappos burst onto the scene as an online phenomenon that combined the no-pressure buying and mountainous inventory of Internet shopping with the kind of service only found in the best retail establishments in the world. Just take its shoe department: a quick look at Zappos' online store gives you a sense of walking into a retail store, except the company has more than 10,000 shoes instead of hundreds to choose from. The voluminous, well-organized site includes a video describing each shoe like a salesman at the mall, except this one won't try to convince you to buy a pair. And then there's the kicker: free delivery—and free return. Zappos wants you to try out shoes in the comfort of your own home, then send them back and try again. We've even heard the store has offered free overnight shipping to regular customers when they've signed up only for regular free shipping, which still arrives in a few days.

Ask a stranger on the street about Zappos today, and if he pays attention to business or shoes, he knows about Zappos and what makes the store so memorable: its people know what need they're filling. As Trader Joe's trains every teammate, every employee at Zappos receives four weeks in the core value of "Wow" customer service; where Trader Joe's asks crew members to leave after 30 days if they're not having fun, Zappos originally paid $2,000 at the end of the first week of training to any employee to leave if he or she wasn't psyched to create the best experience a customer ever had. (The offer is now $3,000 since Amazon bought Zappos for stock in the range of $1 billion.)

You could set up a website today and sell the same shoes Zappos does; it's the experience of buying that Zappos really helps each teammate cultivate with every customer. The thorough training and transparent expectations from the management team makes what Zappos does clear, and the "how" is emphasized from the first interview. One of Zappos' values is "Create fun and a little weirdness." They ask new employees how weird they are. If you don't know how weird you are or what makes you unique, then you don't get hired. Because Zappos' reps don't have scripts, they hire people with clear personalities and who love to share them with customers. The result is a unique buying experience: customers keep going back to fill their need for shoes and their need for a relationship with a company they trust.

How Do You Define Success?

People want to do their best. They can't when they don't know where they're going (goals), what they do that's unique (strategy), or how to measure their efforts (benchmarks). A football player who doesn't know that his team is trying to get into the end zone is just a man in a uniform running around in the grass. A football player who doesn't know that his team is trying to be the best passing team won't be too helpful if he spends all his time imagining new running plays. When the best football players can all lift 225 pounds 20 times while our gridiron giant can only lift that much for 15 reps, not knowing what the other players can do will keep getting him thrown face-first into the turf without knowing why.

Every teammate needs to be clear on how you as a leader and your organization define success. When Jack Welch led

General Electric, he had a simple little goal for the company: be the most competitive enterprise on earth. Other than the Roman Empire's wanting to make the whole world part of it, there may never have been a more clearly stated goal. That said, it wasn't as clear as Welch's strategy, which was also his benchmark to see how each business was doing: be number one or number two in each of the 350 businesses where GE competed.

Compare the strategies at Trader Joe's and Zappos. Zappos' strategy is also its first value: "Deliver WOW through service." Anyone who buys from Zappos knows what makes the company unique. Trader Joe's strategy is slightly more complicated but just as obvious: reasonably priced upscale food for educated folks delivered in a mom-and-pop environment. In a recent talk we gave, we asked the group of executives to tell us what their companies' strategy was in one sentence. Of the group of eight, only one could do so. When we then asked whose company was performing the best, everyone pointed at the man who was entirely clear about his company's strategy.

What Values Govern your Actions?

When your values read like a laundry list, you don't have values—you have a corporate website. The world assumes that you value leadership, collaboration, and integrity; members of every team need more. We all want to know what the work we're doing is having an impact upon and why we should pour our guts into it. We don't express our values once a year in a speech to all employees or deliver them in an interview to be posted on YouTube, although those can be some of the places where we need to express what matters most. We need to create clarity about the way we value working together every day so it creates a culture where teammates know their efforts matter.

Trader Joe's third value, "Create WOW customer service every day," has the same all caps experiential emphasis as Zappos' first value, "Deliver WOW through service." WOW service is now a cliché for any other organization, and Trader Joe's has mastered it because its other values go deeper into what that means. While Trader Joe's may start its values with "integrity," its sixth pillar of how to work together, "kaizen," promotes the kind of interaction they want as teams and with customers.

Made famous after World War II in various Japanese companies that focused on process improvement, *kaizen* means get a little better every day. The store managers, called "captains" and "first mates" at TJ's, work with crew members to make 1-percent improvements every day. Since no one person can figure out how to improve the store or customer experience on his or her own, the value drives collaboration, rather than paying it lip service. It's so simple, there's no way anyone can be unclear about what the organization hopes for from teammates.

Welch used the "Find a better way every day" mantra as well, and then in the 1990s he turned it into a value he used to review every manager: boundaryless behavior. He wanted total collaboration across his businesses, and managers were rated high, medium, or low by their peers. GE had always valued the person who came up with the good idea, but now it wanted to make sure everyone knew his or her contribution mattered.

The values in any organization are never lived out perfectly, but they become the clarity from which teams can act. Zappos will hire and fire people based on its tenth of 10 values: "Be humble." If you treat the driver that picks you up at the airport badly for your interview, you won't be hired. If you get a big ego about all your sales, you won't last.

Playful fact: Jack Welch probably would not have survived at Zappos. That is why we as leaders need to clearly express the values of our organizations: they attract the kind of people who can embody the ways of working together that reveal in actions why every teammate's contribution is essential.

Where Do You Communicate the Messages Everyone Needs?

Organizations come together to produce results. Results don't come from talking about results but from creating an environment where everyone is clear about what produces results, how to have an impact on those results, and why those results and methods matter. Creating clarity with your communication is about establishing an ongoing dialogue with every teammate. We leaders who commit to clarity get the privilege of constantly engaging teammates around how we're fulfilling our purposes together.

John Bane, Trader Joe's current CEO, and his predecessors have all reinforced whom they serve by spending time in the stores, meeting customers and working side by side with employees. Zappos CEO Tony Hseih has an open-door policy: he doesn't have a separate office but a cube with no doors. Welch held town halls with managers where they could challenge him about his values, goals, and strategies. We have to find the ways to keep the conversation with every teammate moving toward deeper clarity about everything we do.

There is no right way to communicate; the question is, are you trying creative ways to show the pieces of the puzzle that people need to be able to put together if they're going to make sense of the frenetic new world affecting every organization? Please don't post a few inspirational posters on the wall and think you've communicated. Don't write one blog post to employees and call that communication. Dig into your experience: remember when you were Jack, the underperformer from the first chapter, just trying to keep your head above water in a new role, and provide the kind of communicative leadership that engages what people really care about. Then they won't stop working on each new puzzle until it's solved.

End Every Conversation with a Reframe

Here's a final clarity exercise that the leaders who people love practice every day. Whether you're ending a one-on-one conversation, a weekly team briefing, or even a town hall meeting to clarify the kind of pieces of the puzzle that every teammate must be able to connect, the question we need answered is, "Is what's in their head the same as what's in mine?" At the end of most meetings, the leader asks, "All clear?" Everyone nods their heads yes. We ask, "Any questions?" Only the brave ask; most people just want to go to lunch. The mistake is, we never heard what the conclusions to the conversation meant to them.

In one-on-one conversations, the simplest way to conclude is with: "Tell me what our plan is, to make sure we're on the same page." Everything from deadlines to details will get confused in conversations, because the way we say it doesn't translate to the way the other person thinks. Or she was distracted. The same thing happens in team meetings. At the end, say: "To make sure I was clear, let's go around the room and review what we're owning and the deadlines." In a town hall meeting, have the moderator of the conversation or the emcee restate what was said.

Never forget Eris' apple. The smallest lack of clarity can create a chain of confusion. Some people process and remember information the first time, others take 27 restatements. Your most talented people may take more time to get clear. Our brains absorb information at different rates, and if someone is distracted because his kids are sick or he simply has too much to do, ending every conversation with a restatement creates the environment where what we really mean and what's been decided is what's understood.

Simple Assessments: What Does Success Look Like?

An assessment is a tool used to gather and evaluate information. In psychology, a battery of tests is used to determine personality type and whether someone suffers from mental illness. Financial professionals have complex models they use to assess the values of investments. Risk assessment is done across professions, from public health to project management. As leaders, we need to do assessments too. We need to gather and evaluate information in a way that clearly reveals the state of the environment and experience our leadership creates.

Too often, leaders overcomplicate the way we gather information about people. Too many organizations rely on scorecards and algorithms to measure everything from performance to happiness. As leaders, we need to hear what our people are thinking and feeling on a consistent basis in their words. Simple assessments that we ask meeting after meeting show that we care about each teammate's experience and give us consistent data to motivate the actual efforts that move toward the results we want.

We're going to close each chapter on the individual commitments with a magic question, a simple assessment that when all else fails, will help you fulfill each promise. Here is the first one that produces the kind of clarity that a team could live off for years. It works one-on-one, in small meetings, or in large groups:

What does success look like?

Imagine if every leader, as we brainstormed solutions to problems or conjured new worlds, asked what a perfect end would be. Any dream needs to have an end that we agree upon, because what we define together as success has powerful consequence: it creates the measurements we use to hold one another accountable.

Here's how it can work. Let's bring back our teammate Jack. You're designing a new website, and he's animated about the design possibilities. He has more ideas than either of you know what to do with. The conversation, in too many cases, ends with Jack excited about everything he's thinking but there is no common understanding between you about what the final result should be. When you assess what success looks like—when you, for instance, define the people it will serve, how accessible it will be, and the number of hits it will traffic—then you leave the conversation with clarity between you.

Just having the conversation about the look of success helps team members understand one another. It creates tangible descriptions of what you really want and makes room for the conversation about why. The value of the assessment is that it keeps us from overthinking how we lead. It keeps us centered on our own clarity, the environment we want to create, and the clarity our people need to know where we're going together.

Committing to clarity isn't hard; fulfilling the commitment is the ongoing challenge. And yet it is the simplest efforts we make as leaders that can make the largest difference. In addition to asking "What does success look like?," add-keep-delete, "The Five Whys," connecting pieces of the puzzle, and Harriet Tubman's creative ways of offering clarity are all starting points for fulfilling the commitment as you lead. There is no wrong way to create clarity, as long as you and your teammates have the clarity you need to achieve what success looks like for all of you.

CHAPTER 3

STABILITY

What Is the Commitment to Stability?

In 1943, the behavioral psychologist Abraham Maslow published an article titled "A Theory of Human Motivation," which introduced his now-famous theory that humans have a hierarchy of needs. The ideas began in his college and graduate work at the University of Wisconsin, where he assisted Professor Harry Harlow in research delving into the behaviors of monkeys. As Harlow and Maslow observed the babies, they noticed that certain needs took precedence over others: thirst over hunger and the need for comfort over the need to explore.

Maslow then applied the same realization to human beings. "A Theory of Human Motivation" asserted that "the appearance of one need usually rests on the prior satisfaction of another, more pre-potent need." Starting with such basic psychological necessities as food and sleep, followed successively by security, then love and belonging, then the respect of others and personal confidence, and ultimately, self-actualization, he theorized that people pursue the satisfaction of needs in a

predictable order. Over the decades his theory has been criticized on two accounts: the hierarchy is in the wrong order, or
the needs he identified are based on our motivations or goals
rather than on our human nature.

Both Maslow's theory and its critiques are essential to our
thinking about the environment we create as leaders who want
to commit to stability. First, we have needs: whether they are
based on our goals or our nature, every person we work with
lives in pursuit of fulfilling his or her physical, emotional, and
spiritual desires. At different stages in our lives, our needs vary
in their priority and what comes first. No new parents ever get
enough sleep, and yet they will pursue love of a child or their
professional goals long before they get adequate rest.

What is absolutely accurate about Maslow's focus, however,
is that our motivations do have an order to them. While they
may differ for each individual, as leaders we have to pay attention to the motivations of every individual, both those that are
unique to our environment where we lead and what each person needs based on his personality and life circumstances. The
commitment to stability is our fierce attention to two factors:
the resources our teammates need if we want them to reach
their potential in their own lives and for our organizations,
and to our behaviors that create the trust that is essential for
personal and organizational breakthroughs.

We can't just pay attention to what needs to get done.
The way we lead, both what we provide people to work with
in terms of all forms of support—necessities, coaching, and
opportunities—and the way we interact with each person to
build a culture of trust, has a definitive influence on whether
people will follow us anywhere, even into circumstances that
threaten our lives, or if they will spend their time ignoring

us, writing blog posts about our poor leadership, and making dartboards with our faces on them.

First, the promise of stability focuses on everyone having what they need—not what we think they need. And as each of the commitments are simple, so are the primary ways of fulfilling them. At a fundamental level, when Jack's not performing, he's probably hungry. You want to watch a team that's been grinding for weeks or months on a project come back to life: give them the weekend off. Our attention to such basics as food and rest, all the way to the kind of training and camaraderie people need, allows them to truly focus on what we're doing together. If we don't notice what our people need and make sure they have the resources, opportunities, and reasons for what's being done, they can't feel grounded enough to focus their whole selves on what needs their attention.

The second, more difficult but just as essential way of fulfilling the commitment to stability, is to build a culture of trust. The words many of us immediately think of when we read trust are *soft*, *warm*, and *fuzzy*, and perhaps our favorite, *namby-pamby*. We realize what leaders who know how to build trust accomplish in terms of tangible results like profits and organizational growth. Jack Welch is not soft, and yet in his way he created a culture of trust where people were willing to spend their whole careers with him. Zappos' culture is warmer and fuzzier, but its leaders are just as focused on growing the business.

There always seem to be a handful of leaders in an organization that are able to create an environment where people succeed and don't leave—an organization where the leaders of the future are born. As leaders we ignore it in many settings because we don't understand it. We don't know how to measure trust, when trust is treated as an unquantifiable concept. If we want to fulfill the second commitment, we have to pay attention to the resources and trust in our environments as aggressively as we analyze our bottom line and product development.

Starting Up a Culture of Stability

Leadership experiment Number Three: you start a new company and want the culture to have the kind of stability in which people want to stay. If you could only do one thing during the first year to create stability, what would it be?

Culture is simply the shared attitudes, values, goals, and practices of a group or organization. The mistake most leaders beginning a new team or organization make is thinking about culture structurally. We think (imagine an overly earnest leader's voice here), "I want a flat culture where everyone can contribute and where innovation is a natural product of each person's unique creative passion." We're using some of these same words and intentions in this book; the difference is, we're making it personal. Leaders can't mandate culture; we nurture it by paying attention to and caring about the daily experience of everyone on our team.

A culture where people want to invest themselves begins with stability, and stability comes from whatever we need to feel safe. Where clarity is about getting our heads right, stability happens when our bodies feel at ease, even when we're challenging ourselves in the most intense environments. As a leader, you have something that works for you, that you think would work for most people, that would make a culture stable from the start. What is it?

Here are some categories of needs to explore:

- **Food.** Want people to feel secure? Feed them. This is our number one answer. Take a group of teenagers away from home on a service trip into a developing country, work them all day, and then hike them through the rain back to camp. What fixes the exhaustion? A warm pot of noodles. Pizza. Fresh fruit dipped in chocolate. Enough said. Please keep reading after you go get a snack. You need stability to learn this material, and so does a new culture.

- **Coaching.** We often think smart people can go into a new situation and always succeed. Even the most brilliant minds need guidance. Access to a person who can accelerate progress by supporting us as we learn and inspiring us when we're frustrated: that can be the greatest difference between a culture feeling stable or unstable in uncertain times.

- **Friendship.** One of the consistent answers among start-up leaders in describing how they create a winning culture: they hire their friends. It can work. If we're going to be spending all our time at work, won't our culture be more stable if we work with the people we like? Quick critique of the answer: We usually only hear about the group of friends that start a company and then actually stay together. Quick rebuttal: Would you rather work with someone you like or someone you don't? Strong relationships create stable cultures.

- **Similar interests.** Another way start-ups create stability is to hire people who like the same things. They ask people questions like, "What is your favorite website?"

and "What is your favorite TV show?" If you like star-
trek.com and *The Simpsons*, you're not necessarily going
to hire someone who digs retrocrush.com and anything
Hawaii Five-O—the original, not the remake. They hire
people who surf because they like to surf or bike or run.
Big companies use this technique to create connections,
and it can work at the beginning of any enterprise too.

- **Praise.** How many times have you heard someone say
  that a boss telling her that she was doing well meant
  more than her raise? Nothing creates security more
  quickly than true validation. Imagine making the
  commitment to telling people on your team what they
  did well every day. It will immediately be a challenge
  because validation has to be authentic or it makes us gag.
  And, it is the cheapest and often most meaningful way
  to connect with teammates and build a culture: we stay
  where we know that we matter.

These are just a few examples, but think about how powerful they are in creating the stability that helps people behave
like intelligent, emotionally balanced human beings—not the
animals all of us become on bad days. The experiment is successful only when you know what will work in your culture.
Every culture is unique, just like every person needs different
things to feel grounded. What worked in your culture last year
may not work now. But our capacity as leaders to commit to
stability is unlimited. Praise is free, and food doesn't have to
be complicated. The secret, as with all the commitments, is
to pay attention to yourself, then the environment, then what
each individual will need to feel stable: that's what builds a
culture where people love to be and can consistently be their
best.

Do You Have Stability?

Stability begins when we have what we need and when we trust the people around us and our organization's direction. Here are four questions to reflect on:

1. **Do I have the resources I need to be successful?** Being clear on what needs to be done and not having the means to do it is like repeatedly hitting your head against the wall. Don't do that. Instead, what do you need personally to be your best? If you're frustrated, your team will be frustrated. We have to know what we need so that we can either find the resources or know we can't have them and get creative.

2. **Do I trust my people?** If we don't trust our people, we don't engage them in the work that matters. We spend more time working around them than with them. Multitasking research at Stanford University has proved that our brains can only focus on one thing at once. We can't focus on compensating for teammates and what we need to do as leaders. Ultimately, there is no teamwork without trust.

3. **Do my people trust me?** If they don't trust you, there is no environment for them to come to you for help, to really pull apart ideas and make progress. They will constantly say yes and not mean it, and thus begins the cycle of frustration that drives people away. Do you think *trust* is a soft word? Do you think that driving results is what gets results? Which comes first? Answer: Whom can you push if no one wants to work with you?

4. **Do all of us trust our organization?** If we don't trust our organization, we won't put in the work. We

constantly look over our shoulder and cover our own needs, distracting from the focus required to get the job done. While organizations are made of *us*, culture can often seem as if it takes on a life of its own. Cultures spin out of control when leaders don't pay attention to the behaviors that connect people to one another and what we're doing that matters most.

You have to feel stable or you can never create stability for your team. The difference between a culture that provides the resources and trust people need is that they want to work there and they want to stay, and if success is possible with the team, they will do anything they can to make it a reality. History is filled with stories of leaders who tried to create stability; the leaders we want to emulate actually achieved stability under even the most extreme conditions.

The *Nimrod*

We all watch other leaders. We watch to see how they perform under stress and pressure, and if they are the kind of person who can guide us to where we want to go. The spotlight is always brighter on us when we lead, and the commitment to stability is how we satisfy the needs of those who simply want to make sure that being on our team will be a ride worth taking. Ernest Shackleton's attention and decision making on an attempt to reach the South Pole in 1908 and 1909 is one of the purest examples of a leader creating stability, especially since his ultimate achievement on that mission was far more important than what he originally set out to do.

When he and his crew landed in Antarctica, their first steps off their ship, the *Nimrod*, were a broken promise. Shackleton had been third officer on Robert Scott's *Discovery* expedition that left England in 1901; on December 31, 1902, in their only attempt to reach the South Pole, they turned back 480 miles from the place no human had ever set foot. Because he was suffering from the effects of scurvy, rather than continuing on with the expedition Shackleton was returned to England in 1903 with a hunger.

The *Discovery* mission stayed another year, and after being sent home early Shackleton wanted to prove his mettle to himself and to Scott. Scott blamed Shackleton for their failure to reach the pole; Shackleton, feeling rebuffed, wanted to show that he could achieve what the *Discovery* team had not. As early as 1903, he already had full plans for a return trip to Antarctica, but love and children, a failed run at Parliament, and positions as a journalist and as secretary for the Royal Scottish Geographical Society occupied him until 1907. Then, after four years of Shackleton's dreaming, the threat of a Polish explorer making an attempt on the pole forced him to make his intentions for a return trip to Antarctica public.

As he raised the funds and finalized his plans, Scott threatened the expedition before it ever left England. Shackleton intended to create headquarters in the same place as the *Discovery* crew's; as word spread, he received a letter from Scott. Scott demanded Shackleton respect the McMurdo Sound and the old base as well as the preserve of lands west of 170 degrees as his for future research. Scott was already considering his own return trip, and not wanting to have more stumbling blocks in his own mission, Shackleton reluctantly agreed.

Shackleton had every intention of keeping his word when the *Nimrod* departed from New Zealand on New Year's Day in 1908. But when he arrived at Antarctica on January 23, in the ensuing years since the *Discovery*'s voyage, the inlet on which he hoped to make his base had disappeared from the ravages of the Southern Ocean. After an attempt at another coastal location failed, Shackleton and his crew retreated to the safety of McMurdo Sound. Even though he broke his promise to Scott, it was Shackleton's first of many acts fostering stability as a leader in the two years that followed—the foundation of a success that with many other leaders might have ended in tragedy, as happened with Scott's expedition a few years later.

As the unloaded *Nimrod* sailed for home on February 22, Shackleton and his crew of 14 began organizing their headquarters, which included supplies, ponies, dogs, a prefab 33-by-19-foot hut, and a motorcar. Wanting every possible advantage, Shackleton had creative ideas about the fastest method of reaching the pole, which some people thought were crazy. The motorcar, which helped them unload the ship across the sea ice, would fail on the uneven terrain as they headed toward the pole, but it was Shackleton's deep thinking about the resources he provided, both the provisions and the spirit he created among his men, that built a trust that in a year would save their lives and set a new record.

The trust building began their first days on land. Once unpacked, instead of settling in for the winter, Shackleton made clear this trip was about doing what no other explorers had achieved. Rather than sitting around with the Antarctic winter darkness about to engulf them, Shackleton ordered an immediate attempt of Mount Erebus, its peak being 12,450 feet. Members of the *Discovery* expedition had never climbed higher than its foothills. Only two weeks into their work, they achieved the summit, completed experiments, and collected geological samples that had never before touched human hands. After the adventure, the men returned to the camp exhausted, some frostbitten, and all excitedly aware of their purpose on Antarctica.

As Shackleton's crew then prepared for the six months of winter, his genius in building stability emerged in the provisions he supplied and his simple hut design. While over the years people have criticized his fund-raising and organization, Shackleton created a home for his men in the harshest of environments. The winter months in Antarctica are the spring and summer in the Northern Hemisphere. On the darkest days the sun never rises, and Shackleton knew that if he wanted his team's minds and bodies to be ready for the research and exploring they had planned for the Antarctic spring, he had to create an environment where everyone was engaged and healthy. The first priority of any leader in a situation where people will face stress and danger: food.

He brought tens of thousands of pounds of beef, fish, milk, beans, grains, canned and bottled vegetables and fruits, enough whiskey and port to last for two years, and three cases of good Champagne for celebrations. They baked fresh breads and cakes, stayed up late singing and storytelling, and Shackleton also included in their provisions 2,570 pounds of bacon. No expedition can ever be marked a failure with over a ton of bacon.

The men also needed privacy and activity. Shackleton took care of both. In the prefabricated hut, rooms were sectioned for two, divided by a canvas cloth. While Shackleton had his own space, there was no separation between ranks. They cooked, ate, and worked together as they planned for their attempts on the South Pole, both magnetic and geographic. In addition to their planning, they brought a printing press with them and by the end of winter they had finished *Aurora*

Australis, a collection of poems, fiction, and original stencils produced by the crew, and the first book published on Antarctica.

Shackleton's way of treating his team before the expedition is what prepared them for the successes of the expedition; in addition to the firsts of Mount Eramus and their book, the northern party would plant the Union Jack of England in the magnetic South Pole. The southern team, led by Shackleton, also set a new record. But for the four men who made the assault on geographical pole, their journey would take them within hours of their death.

As the time for the main purpose of the *Nimrod* expedition approached, Shackleton chose a team of four based on the number of ponies that were still alive. Shackleton had favored them instead of dogs, thinking they would hold up better under the strain and weather; only four had survived the winter. They would carry the supplies for the 90-day, 1,719-mile journey to the pole and back. In addition to Frank Wild, with whom he'd been on the *Discovery* expedition, he brought along Jameson Adams and Eric Marshall, who was a surgeon. Perhaps because he had been passed over for Adams as second in charge, Marshall's journal is filled with his disgust for Shackleton and his leadership. Yet in the end, it was Shackleton's valuing the four men's lives over the pole that would become one of the great moments in the history of leadership.

On October 29, 1908, they departed from the base. Depots had been laid out with provisions to lessen the carried load, and the ponies allowed them a fast pace, at first. They needed 16 miles a day to get to the pole and back in three months, but the first pony died on November 21, another was lost on

November 28, and the third on December 1. The pace slowed as two sledges were abandoned, the final pony pulling one supply sledge and the four men the other.

When the fourth pony fell into a crevasse on December 7, the bigger problem than the loss of its carrying power was the food lost down the deep hole. They had planned to eat the pony when its power ran out; Shackleton recalculated their rations and extended the trip to 110 days. Even though they had already passed the distance covered by the *Discovery* crew by the end of November, on January 4, with less than three weeks of food remaining, he realized they couldn't make it to the pole and stay alive. The men were already complaining of hunger, thinning and sick. Over the next five days, they sought the revised goal of reaching within 100 miles of the pole, and having left their sleds, they half-ran on January 9 to the new record of 97 miles from the southernmost place on Earth.

When the team turned around after 73 days, it was the point in which the trust Shackleton had built in the hut over dark winter's days became essential. The way home was supposed to take 50 days if they were going to make the March 1 deadline for the *Nimrod* to leave the continent, and that exceeded their already-reduced daily intake by 13 days. Shackleton cut rations twice more from the 110-day estimate, and by January 31, all of them were sick. When Shackleton forced his breakfast biscuit on Wild, Wild wrote in his diary, "BY GOD I shall never forget. Thousands of pounds would not have bought that one biscuit."

They stretched their food to the very edge of survival, and never could they have gotten so close to the pole without trusting Shackleton. If Shackleton was not ultimately concerned with the lives of his men, they never would have made it home. They followed him to the edge of death because even Marshall trusted him. While Scott's expedition a few years later reached the pole, he and his men didn't make it back. The reason, of course, was not only about leadership. Adventuring in Antarctica in the first decades of the twentieth century, all alone, completely at the mercy of the weather, much was beyond a leader's control.

But the simple fact remains; Shackleton set a record *and* got his men home. When Marshall collapsed on February 27, Wild and Shackleton, freshly resupplied with food by another teammate at their final depot, made the last push for the *Nimrod*, arriving on February 28, in time to save every crew member. Like every leader, Shackleton made mistakes. If he had followed the advice of others, he might have made the pole: if he used dogs instead of ponies or if he had skis to cross the ice and snow. But when it mattered most, when the lives of his men were at risk, he chose a record and their lives over his original goal. He pushed them as far as they could go, and he never betrayed their ultimate trust. This trust created the stable environment the men needed to succeed.

Although Shackleton sent word back from New Zealand that he was disappointed, he returned to England as a hero and was knighted by King Edward VII; and perhaps the greatest evidence of his impact as a leader was that the stability he created produced a team of leaders that continued to explore the Antarctic. Shackleton himself spent the rest of his life on explorations, and when he died on board the *Quest* in 1922, on yet another polar expedition, one of his team was waiting to assume the mantle. Frank Wild, his second, after decades of exploring together, took command of the ship.

Radar and the Alarm

Back to your brain: when our needs aren't met, we feel it. Even if we can't identify what's missing or wrong, we know. The reason: our bodies have *radar*. Through millennia, we have learned to recognize trouble through our nervous system. Our hair, skin cells, eyes, and nostrils sense the world around us and feed that data through the spinal cord up to the command center in our brains. We know when someone is angry just by the way he wrinkles his nose. We may not know why or whether we're part of what's causing his response, but every human being who pays any attention to the world around him can literally smell danger.

When our needs are not met, the sense of trouble begins to pulse through our body; when the trouble is serious enough, it sets off an ancient part of the brain called the *alarm*. Adrenaline increases the heart rate, which pumps more oxygen through the blood, and we're ready to fight or flee. And neuroscientists now know, in addition to fight or flight, that there is a third response to fear, anxiety, and stress: we freeze.

Imagine a lion has just plopped himself in front of you. Your body sees and smells him, sending a message to your brain, which triggers the alarm. Our alarm is not positive or negative; rather it is a functional necessity in our survival. In the case of the lion, we want our alarm to go off. To keep us alive—because we don't really want to die by being eaten as lunch—the alarm in our brain will either tell us to fight, flee, or freeze. Depending on the character of the lion, any of the responses could be the right one.

Alarm problem Number One for leaders: If a teammate's alarm goes off when there is no lion in the room, her body fills with adrenaline—but there's no reason to run. This causes her stress response to go off, and if she's the flight type, she won't show up to meetings in which you need her. If she fights, she ruins meetings with her anger. If she freezes, she is in the meetings, but she chokes, she can't respond when you need her, and others notice.

Alarm problem Number Two: When someone's alarm goes off, it triggers the alarms of the people around him. We know when someone is stressed. When he runs, lashes out, or shuts down, it triggers our own stress response. Suddenly, a meeting breaks into a three-ring circus of panic, although there is no lion in sight. As leaders, we need to know how the environment we are in sets off the alarm of all the members of our team and what they need to put their alarms on sleep or turn them off.

Research is proving that with training, people can learn to control their reactions using the other parts of their brain. Our memories are filled with ideas and experiences that help us refocus on what matters. Leaders who commit to stability have known this intuitively for years. When we create an environment in which people feel secure and have what they need, they can focus on what they need to do.

Paying attention to our teammates' alarms is the difference between keeping them from panicking and losing hours and days, if not weeks, in their fear response—and helping them feel secure in what they're doing, even when what they're doing has risk and truly frightens them. The way to keep their alarms from going off: commit to figuring out what each teammate needs to feel stable on ordinary days and in times of panic.

Recognize Each Teammate's Fear Response

The three options to the fear response are fight, flight, or freeze. The way to recognize them in your teammate: Next

time you see him under stress or in a situation that scares him—
it could be anything from an accelerated deadline to having to
give a big presentation—which animal does he remind you of?
The lion? The rabbit? Or a deer caught in headlights?

The person who fights is like a lion. He can literally roar,
puff out his chest, and he wants to confront the issue head on.
He gets angry when a meeting or project isn't going his way,
and like the warrior he feels like he is, or wants to be, his brain
will fill him with chemical courage to confront fear.

The person who flees is like a rabbit. Imagine a cute little
bunny eating grass in your front yard. The moment the bunny
perceives you, it may freeze for an instant, but that's only
because it's hungry. It's not really freezing, just continuing
to scan the environment as it nibbles, having seen you on
its radar. The moment the bunny senses true danger, like a
shadow that it thinks is a bunny-eating bird, it runs. So will
some of your people; the moment they sense conflict, they will
go hide in their cars.

The final option that most of us haven't been trained to
notice, in ourselves or in others, is the freeze response to
stress and danger. When a deer gets flashed with headlights, it
freezes and there is a high probability of its becoming roadkill.
When people freeze, it's like the case of a wild animal that may
allow a possible predator to just move on and not attack it.
But that doesn't work in a team meeting, when a customer is
screaming, or rumors of a huge change surface. When teammates are incapable of speech or effective action, they need
our help.

When we recognize their fear response, instead of letting
it trigger our own response we can create some space around
the lion until it turns into a human again, soothe the bunny so
it won't run away, or give the frozen deer a little nudge. We
each have different strategies for protecting others from angry

people, keeping people engaged, and pulling teammates out of their own heads and into what we're doing now. It's when we pay attention to the fact that they are afraid that we can prevent ourselves from overreacting and give them the chance to recover.

Free Lunch, No Chores, Unlimited Learning, and Consistent Messages

Organizations have to pay attention to stability as a whole as well. We can help to prevent our alarms from going off by creating an environment where the resources people need are so available, they can always pour themselves into what they want to do. We can't prevent mistakes and the occasional disaster, but we can explore the risks of the system where we lead and facilitate the fulfillment of needs. From the basics such as the tools we need to do the job to the kind of emotional support, either from us or an outside coach, the resources we provide are the first step to proving we're trustworthy as leaders and as representatives of our organization or movement. These examples provide the kind of case studies that will inspire you to think about what needs are and aren't being filled in your organization and what you can do about it.

Free Lunch on Snow Days

At the Hospital for Special Care, in New Britain, Connecticut, patients rebuild their lives after spinal cord and brain injuries. Whether sustained in a car accident, playing sports, or from diseases like Lou Gehrig's, when a patient is relearning the activities of daily living so he can go back to being fully independent, missing a day of therapy can affect progress. The relationship with the same therapists and doctors has deep impact on the patient's ability to heal. Think of the anxiety we feel just changing who cuts our hair. Now imagine recovering from a life-threatening condition, and the value of a team of people who the patient knows will care for him.

So the hospital has a policy: on snow days, employees get free lunch. The benefits to the patients are obvious, but think of the benefit to the leader and the organization. Employees know the hospital values the extra effort the staff makes to show up when there is inclement weather. Team leaders don't have to reorganize schedules; administrators don't have to make up for lost billable hours. The CEO of the hospital gets the benefit of employees who share the experience of working together under adverse conditions. They will tell the story of snow days for weeks, if not years, and that positive energy will carry on to the patients that week and throughout their recovery. If each lunch costs $10 and the hospital feeds 250 staff members, $2,500 buys a level of morale and quality care that, were it not for free lunch, would cost tens of thousands of dollars in lost service alone.

Take Away the Chores of Life

Oracle provides free dry-cleaning and photo development. EMC has Spinning and yoga classes on its campus. Google and DreamWorks serve free meals. Timberland pays people to volunteer in the community one week per year. Why do companies offer these benefits? When employees don't have to run errands, drive to the gym, or go out to lunch, people's alarms don't go off. Instead of worrying about personal demands, they can spend a few extra minutes listening to a colleague, thinking up the next great idea, or learning to be a better leader.

Taking away the chores of life doesn't have to cost anything either. Listening is free. If leaders intentionally book time to have conversations with teammates with one purpose—to hear their needs—one of the most damaging behaviors we all love to practice goes away: complaining. Initial studies have already been done about how we waste time at work and which gender complains more; the data reveal we complain the same amount, we just complain for different reasons.

We don't have a scientific investigation into the damage created by complaining and the time spent venting about everything that's wrong in the organizations where we work, but we can already safely offer this observation: a lot of time, energy, and money is wasted when people complain. While the listening leader doesn't suddenly correct all the reasons for the complaints, she shows that what her teammates think matters, so they know their critiques will be heard and valued, and when efforts are made to fix the problems, the stability stops the complaints in the future—some of them anyway.

Unlimited Learning

In 1995, a consortium of noncompeting Fortune 500 companies formed the world's largest online resource center. With over 500,000 courses, everything from half-hour sessions on how to run an effective meeting to coursework leading to master's degrees based on curriculum from Stanford University and the London School of Economics, millions of employees from such charter member companies as GM, Motorola, 3M, Pfizer, and UPS could quite literally learn anything they wanted.

Want your teammates to improve? They need to learn. If you force them into a classroom, they won't. Provide them with multiple options for when and how to learn, tie that to what you want them to do in their work, and suddenly their curiosity is linked to the production you need. The stability created when people have the chance to learn cannot be completely quantified. The value of ideas generated when teammates have the learning resources they need to inspire their brains is infinitely valuable. We can't force learning, but we can invite people into the experience of learning and provide them with as many arenas as possible to satisfy their curiosity so they will be excited to contribute to what we want to achieve as a team.

The E-mail They Never Will Forget

In addition to food and the basics of life, all of us need to feel secure where we work. The problem in the twenty-first century is that no organization is ultimately stable. Changing markets and the intense competition of a global economy aren't going to slow down. So as leaders, while our organizations may not be stable, we have to be. In everything we do, even as sales and balance sheets wobble, we have to be consistent.

The easiest way to do this is to be the same person you were before the changes. One of the clear ways to know if a leader creates stability is in observing how we communicate changes. For instance, when Zappos was sold to Amazon, Zappos' CEO Tony Hsieh answered every question in a letter to employees, including the revelation that because the companies would continue to be run separately, employees would not get an Amazon discount, and Amazon employees could have the Zappos discount only if "they bake us cookies and deliver them in person." That's the same kind of personality—serious about the business, but with a playful twist—that is Zappos' culture. Hsieh's consistency created stability for his team in a time when they would naturally freak out.

A year after Amazon bought Zappos, it bought Woot.com, the retail site that began selling just one deeply discounted item a day. What you're about to read is not the way a publicly traded CEO would communicate with his team after a purchase or sale. This, however, is exactly the way CEO Matt Rutledge has always communicated. Reading a few excerpts from his letter, ask yourself how you communicate with your team now, and what kind of e-mail you would need to send in a time of insecurity to lead people through the change.

I know I say this every time I find a picture of an adorable kitten, but please set aside 20 minutes to carefully read this entire e-mail. Today is a big day in Woot history. This morning, I woke up to find Jeff Bezos the Mighty had seized our magic sword. Using the Arthurian model as a corporate structure was something our CFO had warned against from the very beginning, but now that's water under the bridge. What is important is that our company is on the verge of becoming a part of the Amazon.com dynasty. And our plans for Grail.Woot are on indefinite hold . . .

We plan to continue to run Woot the way we have always run Woot—with a wall of ideas and a dartboard. From a practical point of view, it will be as if we are simply adding one person to the organizational hierarchy, except that one person will just happen to be a billion-dollar company that could buy and sell each and every one of you like you were office furniture.

Nevertheless, don't worry that our culture will suddenly take a leap forward and become cutting-edge. We're still going to be the same old bottom-feeders our customers and readers have come to know and love, and each and every one of their pre-written insult macros will still be just as valid in a week, two weeks, or even next year. For Woot, our vision remains the same: somehow earning a living on snarky commentary and junk.

If Rutledge had suddenly gotten serious, his people wouldn't have trusted him. If his people then got worried and serious, the organization would have lost the "snark"; what made the company valuable, which came from the culture's way of working together as much as the service the company provided, could have disappeared.

The way we write about change, mistakes, and good news either creates trust in who we are and what we're paying attention to, or we as leaders look like detached automatons with selfish agendas. There is no secret to this kind of communication except knowing that your people need to feel connected to you in times of uncertainty. Be the same person you've been that made them want to work with you in good times: when things are falling apart or changing in a way that could feel unstable, they need a few paragraphs from that same guy or gal.

General Mills

As we transition into the second half of this chapter about building a culture of trust, we wanted to highlight a corporation that goes over the top to provide for the needs of its people and creates a working environment where employees get the experience they sign up for. It doesn't matter which list you go to ranking the best places to work—*Fortune*, *Working Mother*, *Computerworld*, Glassdoor.com—you're likely to find General Mills.

When these lists are released, blogs fill up with critiques about which companies are really organizations where people want to stay and develop careers, and there inevitably are accusations of false advertising. We chose to highlight General Mills because it is the kind of company where the majority of employees actually agree with the press. Full disclosure: we do not work for General Mills, we have not worked for General Mills, and we do not have friends who will benefit from this case study.

General Mills has spent decades creating a culture where its employees have stability, both the resources they need for their lives and the career development experiences for managers and the culture as a whole. We're not presenting it as the perfect business. In fact, before we explore what it does, let's start with the kind of complaints we've heard. The company known for Cheerios, Green Giant, and Haagen-Dazs grew slowly in 2010, with sales, up 1 percent in the final quarter of 2010 and earnings per share that were a penny less per share a year earlier.

General Mills is big, with net sales around $16 billion and 33,000 employees, so it's structure is hierarchical and traditional. Because it hires many of its employees right out of college or graduate school, promotion pools stay full, and career growth can be slow. Employees hired from the outside can have trouble fitting into the culture of teams that have risen through the company together. The company could easily be labeled insular, with a 3-percent voluntary turnover rate among its employees in the Minneapolis-Saint Paul area, home of its corporate headquarters, and 2 percent nationally—where averages across industries can be as much as 10 times higher.

Every complaint we just presented (that promotions are slow and the culture is insular) is also a reason why General Mills is the kind of stable company where people build careers. General Mills was 155 on the Fortune 500 list of America's biggest companies in 2010, up from 193 in 2009, and it was the third largest food products company behind Pepsi and Kraft. Being the world's sixth largest food company, General Mills' size and famous brands make it the kind of consistent performer—its average growth rate from 1999 to 2009 based on earnings per share was 8.4 percent—where every employee gets to participate in a top-of-class business.

General Mills provides the kind of resources that many companies advertise, and extras that make it possible for teammates to stay for the long term—on-site day care for infants, concierge service, oil changes on site, sabbatical time—and employees use these services. It covers $10,000 of expenses if an employee wants to adopt a child. The company's 18 employee networks create the inclusivity and camaraderie needed in a big company. Perhaps most important, in a world where employees often feel like their companies don't care, General Mills' flextime policies make it possible to take care of family emergencies and needs, and taking the time off will not affect a person's career.

Let's back up quickly just to make sure one of those benefits really stuck in your mind: General Mills values life balance. It wants its employees to be able to stay for the long term. It builds trust by really living its policies, such as the $10,000 to help families struggling to have kids adopt a child. A critic could say it's a cheap publicity stunt, because most families won't use it. But if you're a General Mills' employee, and you want a family, it's the kind of gift that not only takes care of a deep need, it's backed up by a culture where you can bring your baby to work and take care of her while still developing your career. In the global recession that started in 2008, General Mills hasn't cut back on any of its programs.

The way the company develops the talent of its employees is just as intentional and supportive. New hires are mostly pulled right out of school; General Mills has a model that takes employees in departments such as marketing, finance, and IT through rotations of different parts of the business, so not only do they gain a deeper understanding of the company, they become valuable to other companies if General Mills is ultimately not the right fit for them.

Every department has a career path for developing employees, and each employee gets his or her own development plan. While of course managers vary in their effectiveness of developing the plans, the emphasis is exactly the kind of support every leader needs to offer if we want teammates to care about their work and know how to improve what they do. General Mills is a talent academy from which other companies happily hire their people.

General Mills is not the model of how you should create stability in your organization; it's an example of a company taking advantage of its business strengths to create stability for every teammate. The company couldn't provide the right culture for someone who wants fast growth. It probably wouldn't be the right environment for a person who wants speed-of-light innovation. But it is the perfect environment for employees who want a balanced life, and the question for every organization is, "How do we create stability for each employee based on our unique business so that talented people want to stay in our culture?"

Why Trust Is Essential for Stability

Trust happens when three conditions are met: mutual vulnerability, fulfilled expectations, and freedom.

Vulnerability may be the hardest experience for us to welcome into our lives as leaders. First clarification: vulnerable doesn't mean weak; it means open: open to what other people think, open about our mistakes, and, most important, open to what we don't know. To be a leader, we think, is to be in control. We cannot control the weather, changes in the global economy, or even what our people do. At the same time, our teams and our organizations are in our hands. What we *can* control is the environment we establish and whether it produces a culture where people want to work together. When mutual vulnerability is achieved, when both parties know they need each other and we value that need as leaders, trust begins.

It can just as quickly be shut down by expectations not being met. Leaders who say what they're going to do and fulfill those expectations—and admit when they can't and tell their people why—are trusted. We know they will make our lives better. We're not saying that meeting expectations falls entirely on the leader. When our ultimate goal is to create a team of leaders where everyone can lead part of what we're trying to accomplish, every teammate distinguishes himself by keeping the clear promises he makes. As leaders, however, we have to meet the expectations we set, or others can't or won't.

Openness and met expectations still won't build trust, however, without the third core experience: freedom. If we don't give people freedom, they can't amaze us. There is nothing worse than the leader who needs us, shows us how to have an impact, and then as we pour our guts into the work, she keeps micromanaging how we work. She checks in too often, frequently asking how it's going. It's worse than the leader who never checks in, because the leader who tries to control us makes us feel unsafe.

With clarity about what a person is doing and why, leaders need to provide each teammate the freedom to operate according to his natural way of working and living or he will pay attention to the interruptions rather than what he needs and wants to do. When we commit to create an environment where we meet expectations, value team members individually, and promote their freedom to achieve in the way that is most meaningful for them, our teammates will trust us. That trust becomes a powerful, contagious attitude with which we produce extraordinary results because we trust our efforts lead somewhere important.

How to Create a Culture of Trust

We can't force trust. We can't make someone trust us even if we want to. We earn it. When a team trusts a leader, it is because they have no doubt that the leader can take them where they want to go. Measuring trust is actually quite simple: pay attention to deadlines and meetings. When people get their work done when they say they will and they show up to meetings when they need to be there, there is trust between people and the direction of the organization. For teammates who don't trust that we have their best interest at the top of our minds or think that our organization is not going to be the best for their future, their work slows and either they don't show up to meetings, or if they do, they don't contribute.

Here are some of the most important ways to build trust that we hope will inspire you to engage your teammates with or discover your own methods for creating the connections that people crave.

Start with a Development Plan

As we talked about with Jack, a development plan is a series of objectives and goals with the actions clearly laid out, both what he'll do and how we'll support him, to help a person achieve. Let's go deeper into how to create a development plan your people will take seriously, so this way of building trust will become a natural habit in how you lead.

First, the planning doesn't start on paper. Remember the first two meetings described in Chapter 1 (the five-minute, then the hour-long)? That's your starting point. We have to be clear about what the other person wants and why. To emphasize it one more time, if we don't know the person, if we don't seek to truly understand her, we're just managing her work. To lead, we have to make what we do take her where she wants to go as well.

Second, in a conversation—not on paper or through e-mails—we have a dialogue about the organizational goals that we need to accomplish. In a movement or volunteer organization, we have these conversations to rally the troops and find out the ways to connect each person to the goal in a way that will keep him or her inspired. In corporate America, the goals are typically pushed down from the top. We need to hit a certain level of production, sales, or widgets per hour. Our job is to make these goals applicable to each teammate.

We make organizational goals relevant to each teammate by creating two or three personal goals for each individual's work. These are the things he wants to do better or differently. The goals need to be specific and things that each of you can create a measure of success for. Think of the objectives as *what* you want to do ("I want to be a better public speaker") and the goal as *how* you are going to do it ("I will lead a team meeting once a month"). The key to this exercise is to be challenging, yet realistic. Do not choose goals that you cannot achieve within the given time frame.

The reason: back to those devices buzzing in our pockets. If we want people to stay engaged, the work they do has to satisfy their yearning to be valuable. If we can't make that happen, they have a social network at their fingertips that will pull them toward another place: to work, to use their talent, or to offer their volunteer time. "Engagement" is being talked about in HR circles as if it were something a computer program can solve. It simply isn't that complicated: every leader has to make everything we do help our people get closer to what they want. That is the most stable ground we can create for any person.

Once we have goals and a time frame, then comes the tough part of self-assessing what we're good at and how we could be better. Once you believe the goals are achievable, and that they apply to what it is you're trying to accomplish together, then you're ready to put it on paper, capturing:

- What you want to do (objective)
- How you are going to do it (goal)
- What you need to be successful (resources)
- How you will both know it's working (measurement)
- When you will review to ensure it's working, or alter plans (time frame)

Up until now you've had informal, guided discovery through conversation. This is the time to get very structured and document the criteria above, as it will come into play during your regular interactions to measure progress. It is in measuring our progress that we keep people motivated, whether we're trying to keep our neighborhood safe or raise profits.

The development plan is the foundation of our relationship going forward, both what we reference when things aren't going well and the road map we look at to verify that we've reached goals worth celebrating. Trust falls apart in organizations when we have conversations and then over time, our memories change. We think we asked someone to do something and made clear how we want it done, and then it doesn't happen. The development plan is the collective memory that keeps every teammate clear and stable as we achieve together.

Offer Regular Updates

If we want teammates to trust us, we have to keep them in the loop. There are few things that cause insecurity quicker than not having information. Here is the simplest mistake made by leaders, executive teams, and boards everywhere: they go behind closed doors and then come out without providing the conclusions from their discussions and how it will affect what will happen next. Of course, leaders need to have private conversations. Of course, executive teams and boards need to keep some plans and strategies to themselves when the information is proprietary or talking openly about what's going to happen could incite panic or cause the initiative to fail.

And, as human beings, we are driven by the gratification that what we do is working. As leaders, as we said in Chapter 1, we are each teammate's personal GPS system. As the systems in our vehicles rely on coordinates to determine where we are and where we want to go, we have to provide our people with constant updates so they can stay on the right path. That doesn't mean they need to have every piece of information in our heads; it necessitates that they have the information they need to trust that we're not going to surprise them and sink their ship.

A classic example that throws most leaders: layoffs. When there is going to be a change in the organization, it will cause anxiety. The anxiety is inevitable. Go behind closed doors and come out without talking to people about what they need to do to be part of the team, and everyone will panic. Whether at a weekly one-on-one or a companywide meeting where people can ask questions, we have to keep people connected to what's happening so they can be valuable participants. Regular updates about the information people need to be their best is an easy way to create the trust essential for stability; or conversely, we sabotage our leadership by not providing enough information.

Practice Tactical Drills

Creating the development plan is a wonderful first step. Keeping people updated builds trust, because no one wonders if his situation is going to change suddenly. Practicing the skills needed to elevate what you do is the key to making development stick. For example, let's take a look at how simple acts of practice and repetition created one of the most recognized leaders in sports history. Whether or not you are a fan of American football, chances are you know what the Super Bowl is. The trophy for football's biggest game is named for a man who used tactical drills of the simplest plays to win championships.

Vince Lombardi's playbook was one-third the size of other teams when he coached the Green Bay Packers to victory in the first Super Bowl. Lombardi created the stability needed by practicing maneuvers to make fewer plays pay off. His signature play, the "power sweep," was the envy of every team in the NFL. He started and finished every single practice running the power sweep. When a reporter asked him about the play, he said,

> You think there's anything special about this sweep? Well, there isn't. It's as basic a play as there can be in football. We simply do it over and over and over. There can never be enough emphasis on repetition. I want my players to be able

to run this sweep in their sleep. If we call the sweep twenty times, I'll expect it to work twenty times . . . not eighteen, not nineteen. We do it often enough in practice so that no excuse can exist for screwing it up.

There are specific behaviors and activities that we need our teammates to be able to execute every time.

Like Shackleton's team climbing Mount Erebus before they even tried to reach the South Pole, we have to identify the specific behaviors that need to be practiced until they become natural. Too often we send our people to a two-day course and expect them to become experts on a product, vastly improve their behaviors, or become effective leaders and managers. The skills we identify as essential in what each teammate does have to be practiced in our regular interactions.

We have to open and close meetings with drills like Lombardi's, or put practice time for key behaviors into every person's regular schedule. We have to do it, because if we, the leaders, don't promote practicing, as our organizations are understaffed and schedules are packed, our people won't practice. They may even want to, but it just won't rise to the top of their priorities.

The reason drills are so important in our constantly changing world: all of us are constantly adapting. Lombardi wasn't leading his team to become robots, and neither are we. We can't give instructions and have them fulfill the needs for the whole month, quarter, or year. Our people, like the Packers making subtle adjustments to how and where they moved each time they ran the sweep, need the comfort with their core behaviors, so when we need them to adapt, they don't get angry, freeze, or quit. The Packers had the stability to make the fine adjustments in the heat of the moment, and that was possible only because they were so secure in all the options. Tactical drills of key behaviors are how we give our own team the same kind of confidence.

What to Do with Emotion

There's one more section we have to include in creating stability, because if we get it wrong as leaders, emotion can blow up every effort we make to provide resources and build trust. One of the biggest ways to create instability in a team is to handle emotions poorly. It can feel as though some days we need to be psychologists if we actually want to help our people work together. We don't. But again, we do have to pay attention to others with a sincere thoughtfulness that they can feel and believe in, because our actions have to match our words.

What matters as leaders is that we take other people's emotions seriously. Too often, as we try to solve problems, we want to solve emotions. People get emotional for so many reasons, and we can't control their reactions—to what we do and to what they feel based on what's going on in their personal lives. We don't need a degree in social work to be a leader, but we have to take emotion seriously. We have to notice emotions, and here are a few of the ways we can build lasting trust by gracefully handling what people feel.

Make Sure They Know We Noticed

One of your teams has just finished a project, and their smiles are ear to ear. But you just got yelled at by senior management about your progress on work with a different team. Even though this team did brilliant work, you spread a little of your frustration around. You nitpick. You don't like the font they used for the headings, and you tell them. Now they hate you. If this happens once in a while, they'll forgive you; but they'll never totally forget.

When our teams succeed, even if we need more out of them, we have to stop and celebrate with them. We have to validate that they've done something they're proud of. That doesn't mean we have to go buy them a cake and flowers; it means we need to smile too, offer a few words of praise, and savor the good moments together—and cake never hurts.

Just as we can destroy a team by raining on their celebrations, if we don't notice when people are struggling in their personal lives, they will stop trusting us. Here's a daily or weekly scenario on every team: one of your best people, someone you want to stay on your team, cancels a meeting with you because of personal issues. You don't ask her about it until the next week, not wanting to be nosy.

There is almost never a moment where a leader shouldn't at least pick up the phone or send a quick e-mail that says, "Is everything all right?" If the person doesn't want to talk about it, she won't. But if she needs you for a few minutes, you may have just earned a teammate for life. You don't have to become her therapist to show that you're aware she's going through hard times. If you're worried that she'll talk forever or discuss something you're not comfortable with, simply say, "I have only a few minutes, but I wanted to check in quickly to see if you're OK." Your job is not to fix her problems, but to let her know that you know she is struggling. If she needs more time than you can give her at the moment, you can set up more time for later or direct her to the resources that will support her return to health.

When They Get Angry, Show Magnanimity

When people disrespect you, if you don't fall for the trap and continue to give them an opportunity to succeed, others will trust you no matter what. A classic example is the older male barking at the younger female, even when she's the boss. It is easy for us to argue when someone yells at us. As a leader, it can be even easier to use our authority to put someone in his or her place.

It is very normal to want to assert that we're right, to relish the squashing of the person who has been a perennial pain and whom we just wish would go away. And while it's completely normal when we feel that way, if we *behave* that way we're not leading. Sometimes, as a leader when the lion roars, if we smile and show respect for how much that person cares about what we're doing, we show ourselves to be the kind of stable presence who others will listen to when it really matters.

Hold Bad News

There will be bad news that no one on your team can do anything about. The obvious question is: when do I tell them? The general rule in keeping the commitment to stability is, once you know for sure. If there is any chance they can affect the outcome and the challenge to overcome is clear, you want them working on the problem. Sometimes, though, there truly is nothing that can be done.

For instance, your team has been working on the deal of the century. It's a creative partnership that's never been done before. It will fill your entire sales quota for the year, and it's only January. The problem is, there is a conflict of interest with a government agency. Your team is grinding away to make the deal happen, but the new laws may make the project impossible. Our job as leaders is to create stability. As soon as you know the problem will get in the way, your team needs to know too. That's the kind of regular update that builds trust. If it's the kind of problem that you can take care of yourself, that's what leaders do to maintain stability and help their people stay focused on what they can control.

Provide Two Choices to People Who Are Stuck

A final behavior that creates stability has to do with people who get stuck because of their emotions. In teaching, when students can't focus in class, teachers give them two choices: put their mind back into the work or go to the principal's office. Our brains get completely overwhelmed when we have too many choices. When fear, panic, or anger gets into the work of our teammates, one of the best ways we can create stability is to provide them with two choices.

A teammate doesn't know what her priority should be: go through the list together two by two and help her discover which is more important. A teammate is in a rage about a colleague or experience: offer him two options about what to do with his anger, such as go home to get some rest or focus on a particular project. When groups of people freeze in the understandable emotion of a world where so much changes so fast, we can also give our teams two choices of where to place their attention, and set them free to act on what's most important right now.

Simple Assessments: What Do You Need?

The simplest assessment that proves we're committed to the stability of our teammates is to ask the question, "What do you need?" Then, whether we're answering the question for ourselves or listening for their response, we have to pause. We may have to pause for a long time. Too many organizations pay little or no attention to need. We're paying attention to metrics, budgets, performance management systems, and the screens (the screens are your computer, laptop, tablet, smart phone—and if you're super old-school, a phone or beeper that you keep around because, even though you never use them, they remind you of a simpler time).

When asking about need, most of the time, at least at first, we don't get an immediate answer. We have coached people for years, and after literally years of starting out the weekly conversation with "What do you need?" the question still surprises them. They still don't know. Apollo's temple at Delphi had the inscription "Know Thyself." That phrase has been attributed to dozens of sages and used by thinkers from Socrates to Emerson. The reason: we don't—too often we don't know ourselves, what we need, or how to go about getting it.

Enter the leader. We have the opportunity every time we sit down with a teammate or a small group, and even at company-wide meetings, to address what people need. To pay attention to the needs of our people is to create an experience of working together where we can't get distracted. After creating clarity, which is the first way to provide stability, fulfilling needs, whether based on Maslow's hierarchy or on our own observations of what produces connected relationships and meaningful progress, may be the most important thing a leader can do for her people. No matter what we say, whatever our ideas, they will remember if we notice what they needed and deliver on our promise to provide.

So first, ask yourself, "What do I need to have unshakable stability in the work I'm doing?" Don't judge your answers. Some of us need money; others need teammates; and some people need a quiet room to think and create. Now think about Jack. Do you know what he needs? Do you know what your team needs?

Kennedy thought about his crew and made sure they had food and safety. Harriet Tubman used words and a pistol to remind people that freedom always overcame fear. Shackleton anticipated the needs of a team of 14 men and provided plenty of bacon, the reminder of home they needed when living all alone for two years in the darkest place on Earth. What do you, your teammates, and your team as a whole need as a group to produce?

The power of committing to stability is not that it immediately generates results; it is the launching point from which the greatest possible results are produced. Without stability, no human being will take risks. As leaders, when we pay attention to what our people need—providing every kind of resource and the behaviors, such as development plans, regular updates, tactical drills, and paying attention to emotions that build trust—not only do they know we care about more than results, they learn to pay attention too. A team that pays attention to need is ready to fulfill it, and fulfilling the commitment to stability is the only way we can find a rhythm where more of the results we want are possible.

CHAPTER 4

RHYTHM

What Is the Commitment to Rhythm?

All leaders who truly get the best out of their teams, who inspire them to be better than they thought they could be and create an environment where people love working together, generate rhythm. The origins of leaders committing to rhythm were not about people, but production. Craftsmen across Europe at the turn of the second millennium organized into guilds. Groups of carpenters, masons, and metalsmiths each had their own associations providing the labor for diverse industries. These were the first talent academies—part union, part training center, part cartel—and the dominant model of producing and organizing the available skilled workers, until the Venetian Arsenal.

At the beginning of the twelfth century, in Venice, the way ships were built changed forever. Instead of craftsmen coming from the guilds, the government began an industrial complex in which workers manufactured all parts of the ships in an area that ultimately took up 15 percent of the city. The rhythm of the assembly and production was so impressive, Dante included it as an aside in his *Inferno*. He describes a ship being repaired:

As in the Arsenal of the Venetians
Boils in the winter the tenacious pitch
To smear their unsound vessels o'er again,
For sail they cannot; and instead thereof
One makes his vessel new, and one recaulks
The ribs of that which many a voyage has made;
One hammers at the prow, one at the stern,
This one makes oars, and that one cordage twists,
Another mends the mainsail and the mizzen.

Before the Industrial Revolution, the Arsenal and its 16,000 workers living and building around the complex could produce nearly one ship per day.

The streamlined craftsmanship in Venice was the precursor to the assembly line used in car manufacturing. First implemented by Ransom Olds of Oldsmobile, when Olds specialized the work of each employee, his plant went from producing 425 cars in 1901 to 2,500 cars in 1902. The purpose of both gathering a team together and focusing each teammate's efforts is obvious: the rhythm multiplies the outcome; it has the right person ready to complete a task at the perfect moment.

And, as leaders we have to pay attention to rhythm because our minds and bodies naturally gravitate toward experiences with consistent patterns. In music, we want a succession of notes that draw us in. With teachers and coaches, we want instruction that paces the learning so that we're not overwhelmed but in which we're always challenged enough to stay engaged and apply what we absorb. In a complete workday, rhythm is the balance between efforts and breaks. From our heart's beating to the circadian cycles of when we eat and sleep, we need rhythm in everything we do to make it an experience we value.

The commitment to rhythm as a leader is about *timing*, in two ways. First, it's the way we organize our work together to elevate what each person and team can achieve on his or her own. Ten people doing every part of a car's manufacture individually might take a year to build 10 cars. Add a leader. The leader commits to clarity and stability for each person, and then provides a flow of work free of obstacles: efficiencies of method, meetings focused on creativity and innovation, and attention to what keeps the team energized so the whole system hums. The leader makes it possible for the same 10 individuals to work together and produce hundreds if not thousands of cars.

The second aspect of timing to which leaders need to pay attention is when and how we interact with teammates. When we lead, too many of us fail because we force it. We demand interactions that make us comfortable rather than stepping back and truly assessing who our people are and when *they* need us to be most effective. We force the kind of production we demand from our teams, paying no attention to the demands of their lives in addition to what we're doing together or the way they need to work to be their best. We even assume the persona we think we need to display as a leader, interacting with people when we think we should rather than intentionally reflecting on how we can attract others without trying too hard.

A leader who pays attention to the rhythm of how the team works together and how to work with the team, on the other hand, has the elixir to relieve the pressure and stress that is stifling modern organizations across businesses, governments, and communities. When a team has clarity and stability, rhythm is the final way of working together in which every individual on a team becomes completely focused on his part of the work. When a team has rhythm, the action happens effortlessly. The leader moves between people and meetings without ever interrupting if doing so won't add value and knowing when to offer direction or encouragement just at the right moment. The team or organization begins to flow, moving around challenges like a river's water bends around boulders.

This is not how most of us were taught to think about leaders. The rhythm with which most of us have learned to lead is more like the sound from an unrelenting ticking clock than an elegantly played piano concerto. We've been taught to drive ourselves and our people to their maximum output. We've become convinced that our rhythms need to follow an external calendar: the demands of the quarter, election cycle, or the school year. We've learned that there is a right way to lead; it is aggressive, directive, and merciless on the march towards progress. Few of us are attracted to leaders who pay attention only to what we're trying to achieve, forgetting that the way we achieve it together matters just as much.

Leaders can identify and build a natural rhythm of working with others that creates an experience of working with us that feels authentic to anyone we meet. Our goals can have natural checkpoints where the moment of interaction fuels progress rather than interrupting an individual's or team's concentration, production, and creativity. We can literally generate an environment where people do their best because they want to. We don't have to motivate people with manufactured competition and incentives. People want to work with leaders who pay attention to rhythm, because we inspire a consistent confidence that puts people at ease and lets them pour all their energy into what they're doing.

The Perfect Work Day

Leadership experiment Number Four: imagine your perfect day. We know: impossible. But if you can't imagine the rhythm you need for the perfect day, your frustration and unhappiness will show up as you imagine, or fail to imagine, what you can do together with your team; as you try to support but ultimately stifle your teammates.

The first roadblock to rhythm is that we continue to think about what we have to do first. We bury ourselves in what we're supposed to complete as leaders, and often we become more manager: taskmaster rather than visionary of better things and better ways to work together. Although most of us get stuck in the management cycle for much longer than we want to, remember that the key difference between managing our people and leading them is the vision we create together, both for our lives and what we do as a team.

The second and biggest roadblock to achieving rhythm is time. Pretty obvious, right? To lead our people, we simply need to pay attention to the first two commitments of clarity and stability in a rhythm that allows teammates to be their most productive and connected to other team members. But we're all doing so much. Daily, too much of what we're doing doesn't get our full attention. To compound the issue, after back-to-back 12- to 14-hour days, we burn out. Although we could quote studies, we don't need to because we all feel it: our bodies—the bodies of every person on our team—were not made for the pace, sleep deprivation, and stress of the modern world.

That makes it our responsibility as leaders to create a better rhythm for ourselves and our team. Here's a quick exercise that will help regain focus and overcome the biggest challenge in that transition. Write your schedule with 24 hours divided into one-hour increments; block off what you would do and how long you would spend on each experience.

We're not looking for you to solve the problem of how to make your day better; we're hoping you can start to build your consciousness of your ideal life as a leader so it will become your real life. If this sounds difficult at first, just wait. Give yourself some mental room for what you really think to emerge from the swamp of busy and scattered thoughts our minds have become. All of us need to reflect on why we wake up each day and take the lead. To spur your reflection, here are a few questions you probably haven't thought about in a while.

- **What do I need every morning to look forward to my day?** Do you begin with a coffee and the paper, or a run? What about the kids? Do you want to have breakfast with them first, or is morning your time for solitude? What about your commute? We don't want you to think about what you are required to do, rather focus for this brief experiment on your ideal. We want you to dig into what gives you the perfect timing between personal and professional, effort and rest, inspiration and action.
- **What do I love to do each day?** We each have the core functions of work and life, and as leaders, we can't get away from them. Unfortunately, we let these activities drive our day instead of starting with what we do that makes us most valuable to the people around us. For instance, you love brainstorming with your team about

the future, but you can't, because all your meetings are taken up with solving crises or planning core functions such as budgets. This experiment is to see if you're capable of naming your version of perfection. As leaders we can end up putting everyone else's needs first, and that can be the right thing to do. Conversely, too much focus on other's needs first can make us the kind of grumpy bear who people don't think of as a leader anymore.

- **When do I have my best energy?** Some of us are morning people; others need a few hours or even the majority of the day to hit their stride. If you know when you're at your best, this is when to plan the most important people interactions or your most creative work. This is also how we know how long we should be working. Some of us stay in the office grinding because we think that's how we get more out of ourselves and we need to set a good example for our people. Some people work like the turtle, while others can produce more in a few hours than they could if they stayed all day. For this experiment, build your day around what you want, need, and when it is most pleasurable for you to have those experiences.

- **What do I need at the end of each day to say it was worth living?** We'll talk about what you need to renew each day later in the chapter, and this is such an important question because many of our answers are habits, not what we truly want. Too often at the end of the day—at least these are our weaknesses as authors—we eat and drink too much. We work more. We fail to pay enough attention to our families and friends. We schedule more of the things we think we're supposed to do rather than prioritizing what we really want to experience so our lives have a balance of work, play, and rest that truly keeps us energized.

If you can write down your perfect day, now you have your game plan for perfect timing. You're a leader, so go start building it. That's right: every day, you can make one little change to get your schedule closer to the rhythm that is ideal for you. We spend so much time as leaders getting in our own way because of the friction of schedules and bad energy. Of course all our days won't be perfect, but what we do with our teams, even if it's working well, can be a lot smoother than it is right now. And once you have an awareness of your perfect day, you can do the experiment with every member of your team and make better days the norm for everyone.

Do You Have Rhythm?

We're not asking if you're a good dancer. Primed by the experiment about your perfect day, we want you to reflect on your rhythm working with others so you can start to build patterns that let nothing get in the way of progress. Here are a couple of quick questions that will reveal if you and your team have it.

- **What routines are working?** With the time constraints and hurricanes of information bombarding us each day, it's very easy to lose sight of why our work matters. Our routines create the groove we can return to because we know that when we take these actions they're our best bet for getting things done. What ways of reviewing people get them inspired and focused? What measurements do you take that keep you aware of which actions really produce results? How are you renewing yourself and your team so they have the positive energy they need to succeed?

- **What patterns of interaction create connections?**
Consistency is key to building relationships in which we have fewer ugly days and more time in which our efforts produce the results we all want. The reason our relationships and our patterns of interaction are so important to fulfilling the commitment to rhythm may be a bit shocking: *people* are what get in the way of progress. One angry, frustrated, or stuck person acts out and our entire team can be derailed. Sound familiar?

Every coup d'état in history can be traced to one person who wanted more power. Every teammate who lashed out probably misunderstood that exceeding their targets once doesn't mean they are ready for the next step. Whether they were in the right or in the wrong, a quick review of the patterns—making sure every person felt that they're on the same team—would have prevented the damage. In every culture, there are certain ways of meeting, reviewing, innovating, and creating that will best develop a pattern where every person can contribute meaningfully without blocking another's best work.

Fundamentally, rhythm is a pattern. It is in paying attention to our rhythm, the rhythm of our environment, and our team's rhythm that we can create patterns of life together, which infuse all of us with energy and make the best results possible. Rhythm disappears when we become fixated on the wrong parts of our work. When we think too much about the results we need, the process that has worked before, and what our people are supposed to be doing, we stop paying attention to what we can do to foster a rhythm that naturally relieves the inevitable conflicts and headaches of human beings working together. Let's take a look at a legendary innovator and leader through the eyes of an equally talented colleague. These men shaped the world as it is today by creating patterns that allowed them to achieve what others thought was impossible.

Henry Ford on Thomas Edison

The modern master of creating a team whose rhythm produced continual genius was Thomas Edison. We know him as the inventor responsible for 1,093 patents; what we haven't paid enough attention to is the ease with which he created an environment of like-minded inventors driven to give birth to new technology. The best account of what Edison did was from another genius of rhythm, Henry Ford.

It's no longer common knowledge that Henry Ford began working for Thomas Edison in his thirties. Ford had become the chief engineer of the Detroit Edison Company when he attended a meeting of Edison's managers from around the country on August 11, 1886. As they sat around an oval dinner table at the Manhattan Beach Hotel, Edison heard about Ford's idea for the automobile and said:

> Young man, that's the thing; you have it. Keep at it. Electric cars must keep near to power stations. The storage battery is too heavy. Steam cars won't do either, for they have to have a boiler and fire. Your car is self-contained—carries its own power plant—no fire, no boiler, no smoke and no steam. You have the thing. Keep at it.

It was the first meeting in what would become a long friendship that lasted until Edison passed away in 1931.

From their regular camping trips together and their winter homes next to each other in Fort Myers, Florida, Ford knew Edison like no one else; the way only leaders who share the same kind of responsibility and success can appreciate each other's ideas and feeling. In his book, *Edison As I Know Him*, first published in 1930, Ford describes the rhythms that made his incredible volume and quality of production possible.

It started with the way Edison worked. When he was caught with an idea, he might work through the night, only sleeping when his brain ceased to function. He ate what he wanted when he was hungry, and besides smoking cigars, his addiction was invention. Edison liked people. "He was wonderfully tolerant—except of bad work," Ford said. When he became obsessed with an invention, he wanted to create a way to maximize what any of his inventions could do. And he expected the same from his Muckers, the fellow inventors he hired to multiply the volume of experiments he could never do alone.

Ford described the rhythmic process of the "Wizard from Menlo Park" in a detail perhaps none of us could grasp as deeply as the man who himself figured out how to perfect the assembly line for mass automobile production.

His procedure is always the same. First he determines his objective—exactly what he wants to accomplish. He may start to improve some crude device already in existence, as he did with the telephone, typewriter, dynamo and scores of other bits of apparatus; or again, there may be nothing in existence to improve. In any case he first gets before him all that is known on the subject, testing each bit of knowledge as he goes along.

Sometimes he makes the tests himself but usually he states what he wants on a sheet of yellow paper in his own handwriting and sends it on to an assistant. The assistants record in notebooks the results of each of their tests and these books are turned in to Mr. Edison each evening. The notes mean more to Mr. Edison than to anyone else, for he knows exactly what he is after and the assistant does not always know.

If the experiments do not turn out as he expects, he writes further notes and suggestions; if the experiments show that they are not worth continuing, then Mr. Edison takes another line. He is always in control.

Edison's rhythm started with the first commitment to clarity. He had a clear objective, and he had explicit instructions for how he wanted experiments handled. None of his Muckers could be in doubt about the goal and their role in the process. That's how Edison produced volume: he took his ideas and then handed them off to others in a fashion so clear that their failures and successes could move the creation further along.

Ford then describes Edison's clear process with teammates that created stability.

Mr. Edison almost never gives verbal instructions because he finds it easier and quicker to write or to draw than to talk and he writes by hand instead of dictating because he can write with the utmost plainness and in faster time than he can dictate. If there is anything to be made or an experiment is to be conducted in a certain way, he draws a diagram in such clear, quick fashion that no further explanation is necessary. The speed with which Mr. Edison does all this is remarkable. He sketched the model of his first phonograph in less than five minutes.

Thus, although utterly without formality of any kind, there is actually a record of everything that goes on in the laboratory and Edison has been able, through this ability, to give rapid and explicit written instructions or drawings, to carry on a number of important and entirely unrelated investigations at the same time. I have never known him to be working on only one thing. Even when he was in the midst of his work on the incandescent lamp, he was carrying forward several other lines of investigation of the highest importance.

In the same way a development plan creates stability for our teammates, Edison had a clear plan for every invention. The written instructions became a permanent record of everything they were doing, so no effort was lost.

The environment of clarity and stability he created allowed a rhythm that had both the timing of how he had people working and the way he worked with people. Edison got the best from his Muckers because he created a distinct rhythm of how he would engage them. He would take suggestions, and each man knew when to bring them: when they were well thought out and applied to the project.

The absolute direction of all these investigations is with him. He is the leader and no one ever questions his leadership. I believe it is rarely possible for any assistant to get ahead of him on a suggestion—not because he is unwilling to receive suggestions but because in his comments on any experiment he invariably covers the point of the subject so thoroughly that the assistant discovers that his suggestion was only a tiny section of what Mr. Edison already had in mind.

He does not have to assert leadership. It is simply unquestioned by any man of real intelligence—and Edison does not for long have near him any person who does not possess far more than average intelligence. He will not tolerate stupidity or long-winded explanations.

Edison was clearly a hierarchical, controlling leader who wanted things done his way. And, in his style, he created a pattern of interactions where people knew exactly how to work to produce the most discoveries, and how to interact with him so they could gain the benefit of his experience and creativity.

The rhythm with which Edison and his Muckers worked became so precise that discoveries became almost inevitable. As Ford said in concluding his thoughts about Edison's process,

> There is no luck whatsoever in anything that Edison does . . .
> He regards an experiment simply as an experiment. If he does not get the results that he planned for, then the experiment has taught him what not to do and gradually, by a process of elimination, he finds what to do.

Edison is celebrated for his patents and the fact that he started General Electric. Many of his Muckers became brilliant inventors in their own right. Perhaps his biggest discovery as a leader: he set up the rhythm of his operations and his interactions so that every effort went into invention.

Edison created an environment that fulfilled all three commitments. The boundaries in which Muckers worked were strict, but entirely clear. The hours could be long—Muckers fell asleep on their books—but Edison was right next to them providing the resources they needed and building the trust that came from constantly mucking on experiments himself. As a result, they created a flow of effort that produced nearly 5,000,000 pages of notebooks and papers housed at Rutgers University. Both of his labs are now permanent memorials to mastering a leader's commitment to rhythm. Ford actually moved Edison's first lab in Menlo Park to Michigan, where it is preserved today. His larger West Orange, New Jersey lab, where he worked until his death, is a national park where all of us can go and witness how he drove a rhythm of innovation that reached the heights of what human beings can produce.

The Foundation of Rhythm Is Freedom

Barry Schwartz, in his book *The Paradox of Choice*, writes about the social science discovery that as our world interconnects and global competition gives us myriad choices in most parts of our lives—from what to do for a career to where to eat for dinner—freedom without boundaries is dangerous. Too much freedom, too many choices: we freeze—even the lion and the rabbit freeze. And, at the same time, without freedom, our teammates will feel trapped. We have to give our people freedom or else they cannot work in a way that is natural to the timing of their bodies and minds.

The freedom we're talking about, however, is not giving someone an assignment and then expecting it to be done on time. When Welch made "boundaryless behavior" a measurable value at GE, he didn't mean for employees to do anything they wanted, whenever they wanted. Once leaders have committed to the clarity of what we're doing, why, and by whom, and once we've created the stability of resources and built the trust of the team, we must make room for people to work in their own ways.

The best way to give people the freedom that begins our commitment to rhythm is actually to fulfill the first two commitments to clarity and stability. Edison had specific requirements of what he wanted from his Muckers and how he wanted them to document their experiments. He gave them all the resources they needed at his labs. Only then, once they had a clear and stable project, would he set them free to work in whatever way was best for their process of discovery.

Another way to offer freedom: companies such as Google and Lego allow employees 20 percent of their time to work on a project that relates to the company but that may be outside the teammate's core responsibility. That doesn't mean a person doesn't have a clear job to do and a development plan to follow; it means every manager wants every teammate to lead within the organization based on what interests him or her most. We want our people to see a better way of doing things and to make it happen because they are not only working on becoming leaders, but because they are also filling voids in what we do that only their unique perspective can recognize and solve.

We have to give every teammate freedom, because when we control people we actually lose control. We not only make our teams more inefficient, because unhappy people spend hours a day distracted or complaining, but we also interrupt the flow of their creativity that is essential for deep innovation and relationships. When we find ways to offer people freedom within clear boundaries, that's when they want to work on their projects and they want to give their best to us as leaders.

Happiness Equals Rhythm

The brain: round three. The commitment to rhythm is about removing the barriers to progress, and it is ultimately about creating teams that are happy to work together. Happiness is not psychobabble. In the quest for results, the way we interact on a regular basis either improves our state of mind or it makes us miserable. Sounds like an easy fix, right? Just start being happier and everything will fall in line. If it is that simple, why don't most leaders pay attention to happiness?

Since the beginning of the civilized world, humans have equated happiness with pleasure: we're happy when we feel good. But psychologists working off Maslow's realization—that the people who achieve the most amazing things share similar positive attributes—have gone deeper into what happiness truly means. Researchers such as Martin Seligman at the University of Pennsylvania and Daniel Gilbert at Harvard continue to explore the positive traits in human beings, which make happiness a sustainable reality.

This is all about using our gray matter to get bigger results. Too often as leaders, we were taught that if we drive people hard and push them to a place of discomfort, we'll achieve more and grow faster. That may be true—at first. But as a car runs out of gas, so will we. Intuitively, we know happy teams produce better results because they don't get in one another's way; they work together smoothly and as a result, more effectively. But the reason we haven't paid attention to rhythms that create happiness for our teammates: we don't know what happiness actually is.

Seligman's theory is that pleasure is just the first stage in tapping our brain's pleasure center. In addition to pleasure, we also need engagement and meaning. Engagement is the place of complete absorption in what we're doing. Written about first in 1991 by Mihaly Csikszentmihalyi in his book, *Flow: The Psychology of Optimal Experience*, engagement is the place where the outside world disappears. It's the experience of peak performance where our mind and body focus entirely on what we're doing. It's that zone of focus where nothing distracts us. But as pleasure is not enough to keep most people happy for long, the problem with a life of engagement is that none of us can stay there permanently. We all get tired.

When fatigue takes over our bodies, it is Seligman's third stage of happiness, meaning, that makes life worth living. Meaning comes from having a higher purpose to the work we're doing. It means discovering a core motivation that allows our bodies to tolerate discomfort, to move in and out of engagement, and to know that all levels of experience lead to something bigger. We need to know that our brains crave all three stages of happiness, and as a result, the rhythms we establish for our teams need to engage all three varieties of happiness.

In addition to the three stages of happiness, leaders have to take into account the fundamental learning of Gilbert's research highlighted in his 2007 book, *Stumbling on Happiness*: people don't know what makes them happy. We think we do. We think the greener grass or the leader's chair is exactly what we need to wake up smiling. Too often, we may not be right. That's why as leaders we have to pay attention to when and how our teammates get stuck. When they told us what they wanted, they may have been telling us what we wanted to hear. They may not know what they want, and they need our help to figure it out. Even once we achieve happiness, Gilbert's discovery is crucial to leadership because we have to be ready to create new rhythms—over time what will energize a person's brain with happy chemicals will change.

Leaders who ignore happiness like Scrooge, because we think happiness is just about feeling pleasure, will ultimately lose the engagement of their teams. While superficial pleasure—like having a pool table at the office or having days off to simply have fun together—can be part of creating a daily rhythm for our teams, it is not enough. The rhythm comes from paying attention to the engagement and meaning of our teammates' needs, and then always being open to new and different ways they want to work on projects with us as their leader.

Regular Measurement

What do you need to measure to make sure that your team is focused? We can create clear boundaries and provide resources, but the only way we achieve rhythm with our teams is to measure our efforts together. We have to understand and be aware of the progress toward what it is that we're working on. We have to make sure we're putting in the right actions to get to our stated objective: if we want to produce a certain number of widgets, we have to know we're getting there. If we set a specific objective and goal and only measure it once a year, to potentially alter the plan to be successful, we're often too far down the path to hit our targets.

Most people freak out when they are measured. The reason: there is no regularity to the collecting of data. As leaders, when we measure performance annually, it turns what teammates do into a numbers game. When we pay attention to measurements consistently and use them to help people develop the skills they need to improve, however, it shows we are invested in their success. It provides the feedback they need to grow and develop. It gives them an opportunity to celebrate achievements and the move toward progress.

As humans, we desperately need that positive stimulation. It can't just happen at the end of a project. We need to see a progression because if we're just fixated on the end goal, it's much harder for us to drive through bureaucracy and unavoidable mistakes and we'll often give up because we think what we're doing isn't working or worse, that it doesn't matter. When we measure with intention and regularity, it becomes an interaction with our teams we can look forward to because we either get to bask in the glow of accomplishment, or discover where we need to learn and become better.

The mistake many organizations make is they measure too much, and often the wrong things. As valuable as balanced score cards and detailed metrics can be, there are only a few key numbers we need to keep our eyes on to make sure the whole team is moving in the right direction and here's a hint— it's not all about sales and savings. Sure, sounds crazy as you're trying to run a business, and profits are the bottom line.

What is often overlooked is that the key drivers to that bottom line are your people. Airline pilots have more instruments these days than they can ever truly focus on. Every pilot still goes back to the fundamental measurement of whether they are flying straight and level: a part of the airplane and the horizon. By checking that simple relationship, they can keep going in the right direction; as leaders, we need to choose the simple measurements for our team and each teammate, which keep us aware that what we're doing is working and that our present rhythm is worth repeating. The key to rhythm is the timing of consistent repeatable patterns, and our people need to know that their patterns are worth repeating.

If you had to pick only two things to measure with your people every day or week, the equivalent of the pilot using the horizon and a part of the airplane to stay level, what would they be? You know you've picked the right metrics when your team is excited to get the numbers, and consistently motivated to improve poor numbers and make good numbers even better.

The Three Levels of Rhythm

In organizations too, rhythm is about timing, and that timing shows up in three distinct forms: function, inspiration, and a new category we'd like to introduce, cadence.

The first level of rhythm is *function*. It pays homage to the methodological greatness of the industrial innovations by the Venetian Arsenal, by leaders like Henry Ford, and companies such as Xerox and Motorola. As leaders, we have to pay attention to the process around us. It is not all that matters in creating a team, but as shown by the inefficiencies of the guild system that led to the development of the Arsenal and the demand for cars that produced the assembly line, we need to find the places where we can do things in a new rhythm that maximizes what our teams can do.

We all want efficiency because it produces better results, and because it feels better as a team. We don't want people to worry about reinventing the wheel; we want them to use the inventions and ways of working that we know are effective to create the next innovations that make our organizations soar. When it comes to the individual performance, Xerox sales training is legendary for teaching people functional tasks so consistently that every person who learns the company's ways of selling can call up the behaviors—the common understanding and language—and apply them to selling anything.

The model was developed by a Cambridge, Massachusetts company and purchased by Xerox. Originally created to help salespeople get over the fear of being turned down, Xerox bought the program in 1965 to take advantage of the growing market for corporate learning. Participants never sold their product. If students sold computer software, they would learn the techniques in role-playing, where they would sell washing machines or bulldozers. The reason: when we learn skills, if we're worried about our product—about what we have to do to satisfy the requirements of our job—we stop thinking about the needs of a customer.

The training taught ways to focus on the person to whom the salesperson wanted to offer a product. Everyone in the class could eventually see the separate parts of selling in the same way that a golf pro could break down every element of a swing. The conversations about selling then became learning that wasn't about understanding method, but perfecting it. When every salesperson absorbed the way to sell with the most impact so deeply that his actions happened naturally, companies could focus every salesperson's attention on customer needs and not just meeting a quota.

What Xerox did to make salespeople more productive, Motorola USA did to process improvement with a system called Six Sigma. Used by corporations such as GE and Pepsi, as well as more than 80 percent of Fortune 100 companies, it was invented by Motorola in the 1980s as a methodology to reduce defects in production to a level at or below 3.4 parts per million produced. That's 99.9997 percent perfect. Think about that for a second. How efficient would you say your organization is? In the next one million interactions with your customer, you are allowed 3.4 miscues or incorrect words, so choose them wisely. That's less than four spelling errors in the next one million e-mails you write. In the interest of full disclosure, using the above criteria, our original draft of this book was far below Six Sigma.

We are obviously not leading cars or robots, but ask anyone who has implemented Six Sigma into a corporate workforce environment and they will explain that success comes down to timing. Whether it's timing of the task at hand (what you do) or the execution of your responsibilities (how you do it), the concept behind continuous and sustainable improvement provides the rhythm necessary to achieve great things. No matter how far off the end goal may seem, taking a similar approach to that of Trader Joe's, where the staff focuses on the 1 percent they can improve on today, continuous improvement creates a rhythm for our people that makes seemingly impossible performance and results approachable. It gives them something specific and measurable to focus on, and breaks it down into patterns that can be easily repeated.

Functional rhythm, however, is not enough. Within any organization, efficiency won't keep most people happy over the long term. The second level of rhythm is *inspiration*. As we aren't cogs, no process can produce the innovations and improvements that truly make growth possible. As global competition increases, the companies that survive will be more than just better at making the same products, they will find ways to help every teammate pour their best ideas and energy into everything they do. We need to be pulled into ways of connecting to our work and one another that moves us deeper than just getting more done. But that doesn't mean that the relationships can't focus entirely on what we're trying to do as organizations.

At Lego, even the hiring process inspires what its leaders consider the key to the business's success. As a family-owned company, relationships and creativity are the keys to its culture. When employees are brought in for their interview, the experience can often be: you have 20 minutes to turn a pile of Legos into a structure that reflects how you will fulfill the role for which you're interviewing. The company isn't looking for the perfect creation, rather the kind of person who can be creative no matter what he or she is doing. Lego knows that the foundation of its success has been creativity and the belief that all employees are part of the family. For Lego to continue its success, each employee must be ready to feed off the inspirational rhythm of Lego's culture.

We need inspirational rhythm because all our work, over time, becomes flat. We get stuck in the same tasks and lose sight of progress, even if the tasks are experiences we love to have. The innovation mentor program at Whirlpool is an example of how organizations can create inspirational rhythm without disrupting their focus on core products. Most of us think of washers and dryers as white boxes that simplify our lives; you may not realize how the industry changed when colors, matching units, and design as sophisticated as a Ferrari's became the norm for appliances. The Benton Harbor, Michigan company is responsible for changing that.

Hundreds of I-mentors, individuals chosen for their skills such as comfort with change and project management, work throughout the organization's cross-functional teams. While they may be designers or chemical engineers, they also make sure the innovation pipeline—the ideas that will improve Whirlpool's products across 16 brands such as Maytag and Sears' Kenmore—continues to flow. All employees have to go through Innovation 101 as part of their training, in which they learn what Whirlpool means by innovation and how the company develops it. Then, the ideas are available to every employee to see and contribute to, or the employee can add her own to the I-pipe. The innovation mentors drive the process across the company, and it's the attention to innovation that creates the inspiration. When it's always part of your life, it becomes part of every teammate's normal rhythm.

Even when leaders focus on functional and inspirational rhythm, that still doesn't mean every teammate feels connected to what he's doing. The ultimate level of rhythm on any team is *cadence*. Cadence is the consistent sequence or timing that produces the highest level of performance a team is capable of. If a cyclist on an uphill climb doesn't keep a consistent cadence, it takes multiple times longer to reach the pinnacle. Inconsistent cadence means we expend energy and effort in bursts. The extra work needed to produce short bursts wears us out, while if we can approach what we do with a consistent rhythm, we can physically and mentally adapt to do more of whatever we hope to achieve.

In leadership, however, cadence is not actually something you do; rather, it's a result of our attitude. The only way to achieve cadence with your team is to believe that every action they take builds upon one another's work. Cadence happens, like bikers flowing for 100 miles at 35 miles an hour by taking turns in the lead, when pure collaborative acceptance of one another happens in a team. Teams can literally fly as they are, no longer trapped by their roles or perceived limitations within the process; when there is nothing in the way of what we do together; when our work has pleasure, engagement, and meaning; and when we have the right freedom and measurements.

Here's the problem: we can't give you an organizational example of cadence because no company will ever reach it. That doesn't mean that your team cannot achieve it; it means that entire organizations are typically made up of a mix in which some teams achieve it on occasion and others never do. Edison's Muckers didn't all stay with him because his drive for innovation burned some of them out. Xerox nailed the process of selling in the 1970s, but almost went bankrupt in 2000.

As we said earlier, we are not leading machines and we are all human beings. While the emotion and intellect we contribute is a benefit, that also means our human imperfections will always get in the way. In the fatigue and resulting emotion of working in a constantly changing world, we will lose our vision about the most productive ways to work together and as leaders, when and how to interact with teammates. Cadence is the hardest thing to achieve and one of the easiest to lose focus on when we find ourselves in challenging times.

And cadence is still the goal we aspire to. As an individual biker will be crushed in any tour by a team working together, a team that builds on one another's work will always outperform a single leader telling others what to do. When we pay attention to generating a rhythm where everything we do builds on every other person's work, we find places every day to remove the distractions and disruptions that block our flow. The more cadence we find, the bigger results we can produce—and the happier we are as a team.

Weekly Reviews

One way to build cadence is by having weekly reviews. The custom in most organizations is to have yearly reviews. Tied to our budget processes, we get in a pattern of holding teammates accountable once each circle of the sun, and it is the silliest process for developing rhythm that was ever conceived in the history of organizational behavior. When reviews are conducted only annually, not only do we miss the opportunity to truly build talent, we have just turned our performance management cycle into a numbers game. Painting by numbers is fun for a 3-year-old with a limited attention span, but not so much for a 33-year-old with career aspirations.

If you take a quick informal poll among colleagues and friends on what the term *annual review* means to them, one of the most common words associated with it would be *bonus*. Even worse, if an employee doesn't receive the bonus she thinks she deserves (and we all aim high), she may shut down and with her disengagement, any chance of development in the near future is stifled. Why? Because without a consistent review of her progress, she feels sucker punched when she was told that she wasn't performing at the same level she perceived herself reaching.

When we think about weekly reviews, it is the opportunity to shift from cold, calculated numbers back to the most important asset on our balance sheet, our teams. Once they have a development plan and we commit to the stability of constant updates, weekly reviews provide a steady stream of data for us to plan our days and adapt to whatever comes our way. Don't be afraid that weekly reviews will interrupt rhythm—it's actually the opposite. We need to know where we stand at all times and that we are working on the right things to make progress on our goals.

Want a way to check in that won't disrupt the work you do together? Take the actions of the development plan and have a simple conversation building on two simple questions: What went well? What needs work? Start with what went well, because we need a positive frame to keep people's alarms from sounding and to keep them focused on what's possible. Leaders get in the rhythm of being clear and creating stability around the good news to set the tone for solving problems. When we know we've done great things, we're ready to work on our growing edges. Then talk about the challenges. This is not a punitive conversation; rather, you're trying to discover the places where different actions will produce better results. We need to build trust in the development process, and that happens only when people return regularly to the good they're doing.

Have the person take down the notes of the conversation, the new tasks and approaches, and keep an e-mail record. Just providing a regular measurement in a few key areas gives us quantitative data to track our progress and stay focused; however, the record of weekly reviews with the detailed notes of our actions gives us a qualitative understanding of where we're succeeding, what's broken, and how together as a team we'll get into a rhythm that moves us closer to our goals.

Renewing Rituals

Once we have freedom, consistent measurement, and regular reviews, a final place we hope you'll commit to rhythm is how you renew. We can't maintain cadence without enough energy; the ways we recharge each hour, day, week, and year will decide whether we become the kind of leader who others want to work with, or the kind of grumpy bear who snaps, yells, and fails our teammates.

The case study is short and obvious: You traveled all week, you arrive home Thursday night just before midnight, and you're already in the office again Friday morning at seven. You saw your children asleep and left before they woke up. You send your team home early for the weekend because they did so well while you were gone, but one of your most faithful colleagues stays late with you to finish a deal. Wanting your input, he keeps walking into your office with questions when you really need the silence for your tired mind to focus. On the fourth interruption, you snap: you simply say, "What?" He walks away and is gone when you come out of your office.

If we do not find the ways throughout the day and throughout our lives to renew the energy we need as leaders to create an environment where others want to work with us, we will make mistakes that over time erode our people's trust. They won't hear what we need from them, and when we say we care about their development, they won't believe us. They will spend more time figuring out how to stay out of our way than actually working on what we're trying to achieve together. But we can find those places where what we enjoy gives us energy and makes us more appealing to be around.

Jack Kennedy is again an example of both the power of renewing rituals and the renewal trap that too many leaders fall into. Kennedy's positive habit in stressful times, particularly in his presidency, in which he could never pull the rip cord and hand off his responsibility, was sailing. His love affair with the waves and wind began as a child. His family spent summers on Cape Cod, Massachusetts, and after learning to sail at age 15, his parents gave him a 26-foot sailboat named *Victura*. He was a champion sailor in his youth and in college, so when he needed a break as president he headed out on the Potomac or Chesapeake Bay on the Manitou, the 62-foot boat he had equipped with communication gear capable of connecting with Moscow. On vacations he went back to Cape Cod and sailed with his wife and children in *Victura*.

Kennedy used sailing and the thought of sailing to clear his mind. In the middle of the Cuban Missile crisis, an epic moment of stress that would cripple even the strongest leader, on a page of White House stationery, which also include the words *money, Castro*, and *Blockade Cuba*, is the doodle of a sailboat. Just the image of a sailboat relieved his mind in the chaos of one of the world's most difficult jobs. The night before Kennedy was assassinated, we know he was thinking of sailing too. The staff at the Rice Hotel, in Houston, cleaned the president's suite when the news came about the shooting. An alert staff member grabbed a piece of paper next to Kennedy's bed—it was a picture of a small sailboat with a striking similarity to *Victura*.

We need the renewing rituals so that our minds can stay focused in the midst of stress, so we can respond to our teammates in a way that keeps us teammates. Other presidents such as Eisenhower golfed; Bush the younger likes to mountain bike, run, and clear brush on his ranch; and Obama shoots hoops. Business giant Richard Branson swims in the morning, reflects in his hammock when he's at home before business calls, and finishes his day kiteboarding. Nelson Mandela, after years in prison, liked to walk before sunrise and to listen to classical music while watching the sunset. The danger if we don't renew ourselves, besides exhibiting bad leadership, is that we take risks in our personal life—the kind Kennedy became infamous for, that offer us the kind of short-term relief that ultimately cause more stress.

The key is consistency. You know your own rhythm. As a leader, you are capable of performing for weeks, even months and years under incredible pressure, and yet ideally, you know when you get your best work done. You know when you are happy to see people, and when you need to be alone. You know what amounts of food, drink, exercise, and sleep fuel your best efforts, and the kind of habits that leave you anxious, tense, and ultimately ineffective.

To maintain rhythm in the work of our team, the first step is to find the ways of being that renew us. The next step is to support each teammate in finding his or her own rituals. It may seem as if your colleague who stays late every night, is willing to miss family events, and responds to every e-mail at all hours is the kind of teammate you want. True, if she is also physically, emotionally, and spiritually healthy. The simple question to ask her: what do you do to recharge each hour, day, and week?

Last, we have to pay attention to the habits of our team and our organization. Google has beach volleyball on campus. Some companies will take whole divisions golfing. Corporations will fly teams to a resort for a learning event or conference. We're not interested in judging what patterns renew a team; we're simply asking each of us as leaders to pay attention to the patterns that renew. Without intentional recharging, people will never stay long enough on our team so we can reach the ultimate goal of the three commitments: to help others become leaders too.

Simple Assessments: What's in Your Way?

The simple assessment for fulfilling the commitment to rhythm is to ask, "What's in your way?" The gravity that stops most of us from flying is either a perceived or real tether, which as leaders we can often do something about. That doesn't mean when someone comes into our office and says, "I need more budget," we instantly provide more money. Our role as leaders is not to solve everyone's problems. Our opportunity as leaders is to help the people see what's getting in their way; if it's imagined, after listening, ask them to move past it; if it's real, help them create their plan to get back into a routine and pattern of interaction with teammates that produces results.

There is a lovely cliché about forests and trees. The reason we can't see the forest as people is because we get stuck. Our shortcuts are wrong, our alarms go off, or we're simply unhappy in what we're doing. The roadblocks are everywhere, but our job as leaders is to provide perspective about where they've lost rhythm. When Jack is sitting in front of you—confused, frustrated, and miserable—we help him get up to 10,000 feet so he can see what's really going on. It's with a wider vision he doesn't have on his own that we can help him figure out ways up, around, or under his stuck places.

Sustainable results come from rhythm. When we repeatedly help people emerge from their stuck places, over time they learn to measure, review, and renew in a pattern that allows them to walk into your office and have a different conversation. Jack will always get stuck, just like each of us has the places in our work where we struggle. When Jack has rhythm, however, he'll start conversations at 10,000 feet. Instead of having to spend as much time venting about what feels wrong, you'll produce better results as a team because you spend your time using each other's insights to build better cadence. When your relationships can always flow around what gets in the way—the highest heights of following the three commitments—you and Jack are ready to become a team of leaders.

CHAPTER 5

HOW TO BUILD A
TEAM OF LEADERS

The Greatest Scientist Whose Name We Don't Remember

Think of scientists and inventors, and who immediately comes to mind? Thomas Edison, Albert Einstein, Marie Curie, Isaac Newton: the names actually come quite quickly, but unless you are a student of science, a scholar of space, or a fanatic about rockets, you probably didn't think of the name Robert Goddard. Robert Goddard invented the technology for the liquid-fueled rocket that has been fundamental in every space flight ever attempted. What the Wright brothers were to flight, Goddard was to rocketry. His first rocket was launched on March 16, 1926, and he might have reached the moon before his death in 1945 if he had built a team of leaders.

A contemporary of Edison and Einstein, in his time, Goddard was arguably more famous, and his clarity about his life's work began early. At 17, on October 19, 1899, he climbed a cherry tree to trim its branches, and instead, saw his future. He wrote about the experience:

> It was one of the quiet, colorful afternoons of sheer beauty, which we have in October in New England, and as I looked towards the fields at the east, I imagined how wonderful it would be to make some device which had even the possibility of ascending to Mars. I was a different boy when I descended the tree from when I ascended for existence at last seemed very purposive.

Goddard then pursued his dream with the tenacity of all great achievers. He earned his Ph.D. in 1910, did a post-doc at Princeton, and was a full professor by 1917.

From his first public proclamations in 1919 stating that he could devise a rocket that could reach the moon, he was both the constant focus of the media and the prized talent of institutions such as the Smithsonian and the Guggenheim Foundation. At a time when rockets and space travel were the stuff of science fiction, Goddard continued to prove their possibility with flights that started at a few feet and ultimately traveled kilometers into the air.

But not all the attention was positive. On January 12, 1920, the *New York Times* published a front-page article on Goddard's vision, and the next day, an editorial claiming Goddard's dream broke core principles of science that only "Mr. Einstein" was capable of reinventing. While Goddard reasserted his findings a week later to the Associated Press, his goal of reaching the moon produced a sensation that the reason of his science could never break through.

Goddard was fiercely competitive, and the criticism plagued him. Over the next 10 years he engaged in a public debate in which he defended the principles of space travel, as his rockets traveled further and further off the ground. But after a 1929 launch in Massachusetts, the *Worcester Gazette*'s headline read, "Moon rocket misses target by 238,799 ½ miles." The continual derision turned Goddard's intense desire to reach space into a deep distrust of anyone who might slow his progress.

But he didn't shut everyone out. Through the help of his friend Charles Lindbergh, in 1930 he received a large grant from the Guggenheim Foundation. Goddard, a professor and researcher at Clark University, in Worcester, Massachusetts, took leave of his teaching duties, packed up his wife and team, and moved to Roswell, New Mexico. He would spend the next 10 years testing different rockets.

He was a master of the three commitments. Every technician was hired for his expertise in some part of the rocketry process. His team had the clearest of goals: the moon. They had the stability of the Guggenheim money, a lab where they worked together daily; and Goddard, like Edison, was in total charge of the process. They found a rhythm of progress that included both the creation and testing of rockets and the diversions of martinis and cards in the evening. His achievement is the evidence: he was not only the first to launch a rocket but also the pioneer of the technologies that will ultimately lead to the stars.

The problem, however, was in how Goddard saw his work: it was *his* achievement. Over the decades, Edison surrounded himself with talented inventors even if he took credit for their work; Goddard did not work with other scientists. While some of Goddard's biographers believe he was open to visitors, his competitors at institutions saw him as being unable to work with other leaders. Theodore von Kármán, who directed the aeronautics lab at Cal Tech, which was also funded by the Guggenheim Foundation, wrote in his biography:

He was an inventive man and had a good scientific foundation, but he was not a creator of science, and he took himself too seriously. If he had taken others into his confidence, I think he would have developed workable high-altitude rockets and his achievements would have been greater than they were. But not listening to, or communicating with, other qualified people hindered his accomplishments.

Obviously von Kármán's comments have the attitude of a rival, but they reveal the experience of those who wanted to work with Goddard. Goddard fulfilled the three commitments as a leader; he just didn't give others that chance to lead with him.

By not working with others who had the same dream, by the time World War II began, as his funding dried up and he pursued government war contracts to continue his research, the Germans, working as a team of scientists, invented the V-2. The V-2 missile applied many of the same discoveries as the rockets Goddard had been building for decades. When Goddard saw a recovered missile at the end of the war, he accused the Germans of stealing his design. The reality was that the team of Germans, beginning about the same time as Goddard ramped up his efforts in New Mexico, produced an aircraft that would travel 55 miles above the surface of the earth. Goddard, working as a solo leader rather than with a team of leaders, never got his rockets higher than 9,000 feet.

The Problem with Opportunities

What they don't teach us in leadership school is that when we get what we want—the chance to lead, the project of our dreams, the growth of the business we always knew would be successful—the pressure affects each of us differently. The pressure can make you want to stop at the very moment when you've created the environment for you and the people on your team to reach the heights you always knew were possible. The moment a leader truly has the chance to lead, even the bravest of us panic.

We have to create teams of leaders because the better we become as leaders the more there is to do. The panic starts when the days suddenly seem shorter. If you're the principal who shows kids what they are capable of, who pays attention to them in a way that makes them feel a confidence that's addictive, those kids will hang onto your doorknob and keep you late. You will have to fight for them with school boards and in the press, and it can be all you think about. In a town, when you fix a problem, you will get invited to more late-night meetings because there will always be other problems to fix. In a company, if you prove that you can produce, you will be given the most important projects in addition to what you're already doing.

The life of a leader that makes us panic doesn't happen overnight. It happens almost without our realizing it: our life is spent more and more in the places where we lead. We spend less time at home, we stop paying attention to our own health, and few of us recognize it's happening. Then something wakes us up. We come home from a really important trip where we've helped amazing progress happen, and our family not only doesn't care what we've done, they're angry because we haven't been around. We call one of our friends and realize it's been months or years since we've talked, and we used to get together every week. We look in the mirror, and as important as the work we're doing is, we don't recognize the face we see.

The moment we wake up is the moment when many of us give up. Either we give up on living a whole life and keep grinding until we grind ourselves into the ground or we take a step back from the amazing things we're creating. We're writing this book for the leaders of today and the rising leaders that are our world's future. Hurting our bodies with stress or giving up are not the only choices when the pressure of too much opportunity overwhelms us. There is a third option.

When we succeed, we have to immediately start giving away the lead and begin to teach others to fulfill the three commitments. Almost always, when we build a new reality—an organization, movement, or a project—we figure it out as we go. One of the fatal flaws of leaders is that we keep all the responsibility on ourselves, and we can't make that mistake. We can't, because our backs aren't that strong and our hearts aren't that big. None of us can absorb all the worry and problems and still want to wake up every morning and change the world.

There is, however, this crazy thing that happens among people who want to build the same realities and do it in a way that fulfills the three commitments: we like spending time together. When we know that we will experience clarity, stability, and rhythm with a leader or a team, we want to work with that person or group. That's why teammates follow leaders from company to company: they don't care only about what they're working on, they want to work with people who commit to more than just the results.

We simply can't be the only one creating that reality. When we find ourselves in the middle of incredible growth or opportunity and the pressure that comes with it, we have to find the partners with whom sharing the load is as much a privilege for them as it is to work on our team. Everyone can lead, and there are people on your team right now who want to lead. Once you know how to fulfill the first three commitments, you are a leader. Learning how to fulfill the three commitments is only the beginning of the value you can find in these three words. If you want what you're doing to rise as high as the heavens, build a team of leaders who can fulfill the commitments as well.

What Is a Team of Leaders?

We admire leaders like Goddard for the way they naturally fulfilled the commitments to achieve unthinkable new realities, and we don't want anyone to limit what he or she can achieve by missing the opportunity to build a team of leaders too. None of us has to work with a team to lead; many individual contributors to their fields can have incredible impact too, as Goddard did with his team of technicians. We simply don't want any of us who haven't thought about leadership in this way to miss the impact we can have if every person on our team gets the chance to develop his or her leadership potential.

We've never really been taught what a team can do together, what an organization could really be capable of, if every person could lead. This is where the three commitments' model goes beyond its value as a simple model of leadership and becomes a world-changing way of building a business, government, or community. Most of the time we think of leadership as something you earn. Whether by an election, promotion, or natural ability to influence others, we think of the leader as taking an elevated position above the rest of the group.

We've been taught systems of thinking in universities and by our cultures around the world that there are two organizational models of leadership: hierarchical or flat. Either there is a chain of command with a clear path of power and authority or the power is shared with each member of a group with equal responsibility. Both models can be effective, but a team of leaders—as it is for leaders stressed out by too much to do—is the third option. When everyone leads, the results produced exceed expectations and occur even under unusual conditions.

On May 15, 1953, at Massey Hall, in Toronto, five jazz musicians gathered to play. Not many people attended the concert because the promoters scheduled it for the same night as a blockbuster heavyweight boxing match. They were the giants of their age, all band leaders in their own right, and deeply talented artists: Dizzy Gillespie, Charlie Parker, Charlie Mingus, Bud Powell, and Max Roach. That night they achieved one of the greatest performances in the history of music, and the set should have been doomed.

Besides the empty room, when talented leaders get together, egos have a way of rearing their ugly heads. It was no different that night at Massey Hall. Gillespie and Parker weren't speaking to each other. They showed up at the last minute and had to take the stage immediately. Parker arrived without his instrument and had to borrow a plastic saxophone. The concert should have been a disaster; but when you listen to the recording, captured by Mingus on his new record label, they behave like they'd been playing together their whole lives.

In jazz, different musicians take turns soloing, leading the piece. In the recording, even though the sound quality is poor because of weak microphones that night, the solos flow from artist to artist without missing a beat or distracting from one another's greatness. They were a team of leaders, producing a set of music that transformed the consciousness of what artists can do together. They hadn't practiced. Charlie Parker might have been high that night, just a few years before the overdose that killed him. Occasionally, different players would leave the stage to check on the fight. Yet what emerged from their instruments elevated the height of musical history, and the group, that only played together that one time, will simply be known for eternity as The Quintet.

The ultimate goal of the three commitments is to produce a team of leaders, a group of individuals willing to pour every ounce of energy and insight into working together. When every teammate makes the commitments, the usual barriers to creating new realities—fear, ego, emotional drama—become the fuel to reconsider how to work together. The three commitments let us look at one another, even people we don't like or struggle to collaborate with, and see where progress is possible.

In some environments, like jazz music, the three commitments are so inherent in the structure of the activity that it naturally provides the foundation for a team of leaders. Usually it takes intention from those in authority. In most organizations, we have to work to make the three commitments the intrinsic way a team collaborates. There then evolves a group of people who form a fluid unit. In each new conversation and meeting, as priorities change and projects flow, the group knows one another so well that different people step up seamlessly to lead a new initiative or project. But teams of leaders can't develop when we never let people's enthusiasm and talent emerge.

The Elephant Approach

As a bridge between describing what a team of leaders is and how you can create a leadership culture where you lead, we want you to feel in your gut the approach too many leaders take—often because of stress and fatigue—that stop our people from becoming leaders too. This is a composite of a true story we've heard hundreds of times about how most leaders interact with their teams when the work progresses poorly versus how they work with people when they focus on what teammates are truly capable of accomplishing and helping them become leaders too. We never want any of us to forget how easy it is to shut people down. And how most of us, when given an opportunity to lead something that matters to us, naturally have the capacity to create environments where other people can burst with energy, ideas, and the desire to bring new realities into being.

A colleague named David had a habit of yelling. On a Thursday when he had to leave early, a key customer made changes on one of the projects that his team had almost finished, meaning everyone had to start over. His people were already behind schedule on two other major deliverables, and when they came into his office with questions that he thought they should know the answers to, he yelled at them. When in meetings he realized how far behind they were, in a judgmental tone that sunk every heart in the room, he ranted about performance and excellence and that they had to do better. He even yelled at an intern for leaving a coffee cup unwashed in the communal kitchen.

When he walked out of the office that Thursday afternoon after seven hours of what felt like worthless meetings, he was already late. His company had asked each executive to take on a community project to build better relationships with local organizations, so he'd signed up to mentor at an after-school program. When he arrived, the class of fourth graders he was assigned to work with was already working on their activity.

They were making models of elephants from pipe cleaners and construction paper. The class had been studying the seven continents, and that day's project was on Africa. As David scanned the room, a little boy named Ernie was sitting by himself away from the group. His chin was on his hands, and he wasn't doing anything.

Without hesitation, David sat down next to him. "What's your name?"

"Ernie," he said. The supplies were in front of him, but he hadn't touched them.

"Can I help you with your project?"

"No." Ernie said. "This is stupid."

"Stupid?" David asked. "Aren't elephants the smartest animals?"

"Yes. They take care of each other too. Elephants stick together."

"So why are you over here by yourself?"

"Because I told the teacher this was a stupid assignment, and she told me to sit over here."

David thought for a minute. "Okay, Ernie. So if you could do the assignment the way you wanted, what would you do differently?"

"I'd make the elephant big."

"Big?"

"Life-size."

"What else?"

"That's it. I don't want to do a little model. I want to make a big elephant that will show everyone what they're really like."

"Okay, how would you do it?"

"First of all, I'd do it outside because it's a sunny day; we shouldn't be stuck in here, and elephants live outside. Then I'd make it out of something that would last so people could see what we did for a long time."

"I like it. So why don't you ask your teacher if we can go outside and make a life-size elephant?"

"I can't do that."

"Why not?"

"She's mad at me."

"I bet if you ask her, we can figure out what to do together."

After a little more coaxing, Ernie asked his teacher. She said it was a great idea, but they had to be finished in two hours when parents showed up.

"Can we do it?" David asked.

"Oh, yeah!" Ernie said. Then, "Oh, no!"

"What?"

"Can the two of us make a life-size elephant in two hours?"

"Maybe not alone, but who are your best friends here?"

"Tommy and Lamar."

"Ask your teacher if they can come with us, and then ask them if they want to help."

In a minute, David and his buddies were in front of the computer.

David joined them. "What are you guys doing?"

"We're looking to see how tall an elephant is, so we can make it perfect."

"And I want to see if anyone has ever done this before," Lamar said. "No reason to reinvent the elephant."

David laughed out loud. After a few minutes, they found out elephants were 14 feet tall. They found instructions for how to make a model of a whale using wire clothes hangers, trash bags, and a hair dryer, but nothing on elephants.

"We don't have time," Ernie said, already frustrated.

"What do you have outside that's already tall and like bones?" David asked.

"What do you mean?" Ernie asked.

"What could we use that's already really big as a base to build our elephant?"

The three guys looked at one another.

"The swings?" Tommy asked.

"No," Lamar said. "It's not the right shape."

Ernie lifted both hands in the air. "We can use the jungle gym! We just cover it with paper and draw an elephant face!"

"That's a perfect idea," David said. "But will it last?"

"No," Ernie said, pouting for a second. Then, he said, excited again. "But it could if we made it out of plastic. Or tinfoil!"

The three boys and David went to the school cafeteria, and they collected all the supplies they'd need. When the other kids started leaving with their parents, they all gathered around as Ernie put the ears on a life-size elephant, and Lamar and Tommy finished off the tail. They'd covered the jungle gym in trash bags, and then used the foil to create its head and a tail. On his way home, David could not stop grinning.

The following day, he had lunch as usual with members of his team. With bright eyes and waving hands, he told the story about the trinity and how much fun it was to help the boys figure out what they really wanted to do and how to do it.

When he was done one of his people asked him, "So how'd you do it?"

"Do what?" David asked.

"Help them?"

"I just asked simple questions, I made sure they were clear on their answers, and then I created the space where they could bring the project to life. I guess you could say I took the elephant approach," David said, smiling. He looked around the table at his colleagues, and most of them had their heads down. All of them wore blank faces, and they were quiet. They were never quiet at lunch.

"What?" David asked.

One of his honest teammates spoke up: "You might want to consider taking the elephant approach with us."

How to Assess When Someone's Ready to Lead

If we really want to fulfill the three commitments, we have to find ways to help others fulfill them too. That means we have to help our teammates lead. Everyone on our team can reflect on clarity, stability, and rhythm, and explore ways to build more of each commitment in our work together. Becoming the person who leads using the three commitments starts when he truly exhibits the desire to lead. Everyone can lead, but not everyone wants to. A team with an uncommitted leader is a pack of lemmings headed for the cliff.

A teammate is ready to lead when she exhibits the three capacities every leader needs: will, resiliency, and fluency. Once our people have been rekindled because of the environment we've created with the three commitments, they won't settle for mediocrity. They still, however, need to learn how to lead. The learning begins with the core work they do each day. If they can't be confident and successful at what they do today, they won't be able to make and fulfill the commitments.

Leadership starts with desire. Will is determined simply by competency in their roles. When someone begins to demonstrate competency in the tasks of his role, when he can consistently do his job, he is ready for a broadening of the conversation about what you can do together. When we recognize the strength in another person starting to emerge, that's when we can begin to nurture him into a leader.

Resiliency is determined by observing their verve: every time things go wrong, what do leaders do? Whether we realize it at the beginning or not, leaders get beaten on daily. We are the lightning rods for the dissatisfaction of those we serve in and out of our organizations. Leadership is not a position of honor, even though it can come with privileges and rewards we think we want when we look at the role from the outside. Leadership is a responsibility which, although it can be rewarding, will test every ounce of courage we have in our bodies. A person is not ready to lead if she does not have the ability to bounce back from mistakes, setbacks, and seemingly insurmountable odds. Leaders always bounce back.

Fluency means leaders can talk about their role with an ease and comfort that reflects their understanding of what they do at more than a rote level. Intelligent people pass tests; leaders take the information they learn and then apply and adapt it to achieve previously unimagined realities. That takes the capacity to learn a common language, whether of a product, a company, or a community and then translate it for each person with whom someone works.

When we see a teammate at this level, comfortable with where he is and ready to fly, we ask the question that makes clear to him that he is capable, creates the stability in the most difficult moments, and begins to build the cadence of what he can do in the future.

First Ask Why

When we believe a teammate is ready to lead, before we talk about the fulfilling of the three commitments ask why. As we asked you in the beginning of the clarity chapter, we have to ask our best teammates why they want to lead. Some of us want to rise in our careers to make more money. Others imagine the leadership role is the fulfillment of a person's true potential, and the position to which every talented person aspires. Many leaders see a need, but they don't see others taking on the challenge or seizing the opportunity, and they step up. But why?

"Why?" has infinite answers; that's the reason it's such a valuable question. At this point you've probably already applied the three commitments to the places where you lead. You've probably already seen a measurable improvement in your own leadership and the performance of your team (or if you're reading straight through, you at least know the next steps you're going to take to radically improve the way you motivate, coach, mentor, and manage). But to keep applying the three commitments, to not give up on what we're trying to accomplish in the inevitable challenges we face, every leader needs consciousness of our *core motivation* so deep, nothing will stop us from paying attention to what our team needs to achieve.

If we don't discover our core motivation and if we don't help each person on our team do the same, we will eventually crumble under the strain. Leadership is too hard: the stress breaks down our bodies and can make life so painful. Most of us simply don't want to lead until we think about why: when we have a reason that is bigger than our pain and when we understand our teammates' reasons that transcend the discomfort of being in charge, we know where we can apply the three commitments to make sure what needs to happen does.

There is no environment too big for a team of leaders who know why what they are doing matters, and who are all committed to creating a culture based on the three commitments that reaches every goal. When we think of the Roman Empire, many of us think of dictating emperors who controlled the world for centuries. And there is an exception to that memory: Marcus Aurelius. Here's Marcus Aurelius's answer to why he led, from his *Meditations*, written in his last decade as emperor of Rome:

> Begin the morning by saying to thyself, I shall meet with the busy-body, the ungrateful, arrogant, deceitful, envious, unsocial. All these things happen to them by reason of their ignorance of what is good and evil. But I who have seen the nature of the good that it is beautiful, and of the bad that it is ugly, and the nature of him who does wrong, that it is akin to me, not only of the same blood or seed, but that it participates in the same intelligence and the same portion of the divinity, I can neither be injured by any of them, for no one can fix on me what is ugly, nor can I be angry with my kinsman, nor hate him. For we are made for co-operation, like feet, like hands, like eyelids, like the rows of the upper and lower teeth. To act against one another then is contrary to nature.

Think your corporation is too big to have a team of leaders? The Renaissance philosopher Niccolò Machiavelli saw Aurelius as one of the five "good emperors" of Rome. Not only was Aurelius the "philosopher king" of the Stoic school, believing that reason could ground the most meaningful life, he lived his belief: he shared power. When he became emperor, although like every man before him he could have led by whatever means he wanted, he chose to have a fellow emperor. Some scholars insist it was because he was afraid of the imperial robe.

What a perfect reason to create a team of leaders. Why, if it's not our strength to fulfill every part of a role, would we attempt to do imperfectly alone what a team can do well together? Aurelius was the kind of leader who could lead with others because he knew Rome needed more than his abilities, and he would be best focusing on his strengths. His "why?" translated into a lifelong duty to see the good in all men, and his lingering reputation is as a just ruler whose character equaled his accomplishment.

Leaders who make the three commitments can fight for what seems impossible because we know just beyond the horizon, the world is better. Not *might be* better, but *is* better. We loan others our confidence on a daily basis because we have enough clarity, stability, and rhythm to plant the seed of greatness in others so that they develop into their true selves and become leaders too. When we know why we lead, we cannot be stopped by the ordinary travails of being human, even when the trouble lasts.

Our company, project, team, or dream might get derailed for days, weeks, or— this is the part few of us want to hear— decades. George Washington lost every battle in 1776 before his Christmas Eve crossing of the Delaware River and the first victory on the way to America's independence. Frederick Douglass was born a slave and lived through 20 years of tyranny before his escape and fateful rise to become a key leader of the movement that would free all black people in America. Nelson Mandela spent 27 years in prison before leading a new South Africa. Susan B. Anthony died before her leadership won women the right to vote. There is rarely a scientist, start-up, coach, or politician who hasn't known deep failure on his way to leading his people to what he always knew was possible.

That's why new leaders need the clarity of why they lead, the stability of knowing their answers, and the rhythm that comes from constantly rediscovering their whys. We want to make sure new leaders have their whys so they don't stop short. When doing vital work, too many people are ready to give up right before their leadership has an impact on the world. When we ask them "why?"—a hundred times if we have to—we help them develop the clarity about what will keep them fueled for leadership, ready to live the three commitments, so together we can reach our version of rocketing to the moon.

The Ways to Build Confident Leaders

When geese fly together, they take turns leading because they can fly further. Cyclists take turns at the head of the pack so together they can go faster. As a leader of an organization, we cannot always be in the lead and we can't lead alone. Once we have teammates with the will, fluency, and resiliency to apply the three commitments to every interaction and once they know why they want to lead, we have to introduce them to the three commitments in an experiential way so they can understand the true role of a leader.

As with correcting performance or creating a team that can innovate new ideas, the process of building a team of leaders one by one begins with a conversation. They are already familiar with the three commitments because you've been living them. They may have already become part of your regular conversations with your team. We want to emphasize some specific conversations that every rising leader needs so over time they can be leaders too.

We have to start by showing the person we recognize their potential as a leader. Let's bring back Jack for one more story, because his character is the classic nascent leader surrounding you all the time. When Jack underperformed, it wasn't because he didn't have talent. Your work in fulfilling the three commitments gave him the grounding to get excited about his work again. But most of us never see ourselves as leaders. Even for the alphas among us who seemingly led from birth, it's because their parents, grandparents, friends, and neighbors thrust them into the role. The "natural" leader is actually the person who had the stereotypical leadership traits—height and strength, intelligence and eloquence, a family history and education—and was told he should lead too.

In Jack's transition from a talented member of your team to a leader on your team, maybe before, he needs to hear you say, "Jack, you could lead if you want to." He'll look at you with wide eyes. He may be surprised, even though you've asked him why he'd want to lead, that you believe in him. It is truly shocking how many people have never had someone tell them they were valuable. All of us, even if we don't like our leaders, know the role is essential. Jack may have never had someone believe in him before. He may be excited or his wide eyes may make him look like a deer caught in headlights. Whatever his reaction, he needs to hear from you that you believe he can lead.

The next step is to talk about how you lead. As Jack's subconscious works on his whys and his brain accepts the fact that he can lead too, in your weekly meetings with him, when you share the way you lead in particular situations, his ideas about how to fulfill the three commitments will begin to pop as well. For instance, you have a new product launch in a month. By talking about how you build your team—what you do to make goals, deadlines, and metrics clear, the way you'll create stability by having regular meetings, and how you'll create rhythm by giving each person their projects to own and have celebrations at the end of each week—Jack will see your ways of being an effective leader.

Especially if you talk about your mistakes. This may be the hardest part for most of us to grasp when we lead. It certainly is for most politicians and executives. If we can share with Jack past mistakes when we've launched products or major initiatives and help him see that we weren't perfect, his anxiety about leadership will drop. We have to talk about our errors with an attitude of continuous learning because when we do, we give our teammates permission to take risks and recover. If we present ourselves as the perfect leader, not only will they not want to disappoint us—and as a result keep their mistakes to themselves so we can't fix them as a team—they will think the role of leader is an Everest they can't climb.

If we share all our experiences as leaders, we make ourselves appropriately vulnerable and approachably human. That allows Jack to see himself like us, and it gives us the second to last important opportunity when building a team of leaders: have your teammates choose where they want to lead. Throw people into leadership roles, and they will go through the motions. Even if they're excited about having the chance, they will lead because they think they should, not because they want to. Leaders have to want the experience, because it is too hard. On the product release, ask Jack, "Where would you like to take the lead in this project?" Match his skills to his desire and then set him free. If he already passed the other assessments for leadership readiness, he won't fail you.

Jack will make mistakes, and because you have a regular meeting time, you've built the trust he needs to come to you when he needs help. Make sure you provide the last and most important part of solidifying a new leader: celebrate progress. When we say celebrate, we mean make it clear that you know he's doing something difficult, he's doing well—even as sometimes he's struggling—and continually reaffirm that you believe in him. We don't have to throw ticker tape parades for every accomplishment; we do have to say, "Jack, awesome. Just awesome." We simply talk about where he applied the three commitments successfully and revel in the results he produced. You'll know if your celebration gave him the feedback he needs because he'll smile.

If you can engage every person on your team this way when they're ready, there is no goal that's out of reach. No team of leaders is perfect. We all go through the struggles in our personal lives and the setbacks wherever we lead that make us less than our best self. And, with a team of leaders, like Shackleton's first mate taking over when he died or Edison's Muckers who kept working even if he fell asleep on his books, on our worst days, our team's best work can still get done.

Our Teams of Leaders Are All Around Us

Hidden in your view are the people you need to lead the work you can't do alone. And they may not be the people you think. Too often when we look at who is on our team, we think of our staff or employees, the people on our committee or in our own town or country. To truly fulfill the commitment to build a team of leaders, our attitudes have to widen. To think of ourselves as leaders is already an amazing mental leap. As human beings, to truly believe we can help others be better requires a confidence and a willingness to risk failure most people simply don't have. That's one of the core reasons we created the three commitments: we want everyone to know how they can lead if they want to.

Even as we begin to lead, however, the limitation we put on ourselves and our organization is that we think only those explicitly with us are part of our team of leaders. When we really see every person we come into contact with as a potential leader we can partner with to achieve, there is a shift in the force. There is a switch from the inherent conflict in the old way of viewing leadership—leader versus followers—to a constant flow of energy where everyone takes responsibility for the results we create together. Sometimes our customers are leaders. Sometimes our supplier, our enemy, or our worst critic can be the person who leads us to more of the purposes we need to achieve.

The power of a team of leaders is that they take us places we can't go alone. Most of us limit who can lead us and the places where we're willing to accept direction and wisdom. We've been taught that when we get the leader's chair, the world revolves around us. Unfortunately, that shrinks our perspective of the myriad ways we can build meaningful partnerships with the people around us. If we think they are here to serve us, the relationship is limited; they can never rise above servants. Even if we're generous people, gracious and beneficent as leaders, we feel one another's attitudes: people who we think of as servants don't give upward feedback—or they don't lead up, because they've been pushed down.

When we're open to a team of leaders, the kind of results we produce can grow widely and furtively beyond our own insights and expectations. The teacher walks down the hall and instead of seeing the kid with the funky hair and the clothes designed to make a statement as a troublemaker—that same teacher can look for the students among that group who lead and make them part of her team of leaders. When the teacher needs students to go beyond their comfort zones on a project or school initiative—or just focus in class—it's the student in the unexpected costume who becomes the best coleader for learning.

Instead of the salesperson seeing each customer as a mark, the storeowner becomes the person we want to learn from— about what products work best for which customers, how to sell the products better, and how to run a successful business. As authors, we've each experienced this. When we listen to the people we think we want to sell to, when we hear what they see in us, and actually ask how we can be better leaders of our own businesses instead of trying to close deals, we create a team of leaders where the deals that are good for everyone close in a way that feels more natural.

Imagine if every politician, executive, and professional saw every constituent, teammate, and client as a fellow leader committed to the cause, capable of leading, so that what we wanted to inspire wasn't one person's responsibility. A broadening of our attitude about who can lead makes it possible for our presence as leaders to inspire more people to take risks. When they see that we believe in them, when we prove it with our openness and willingness to engage every teammate, as a group we begin to produce the kind of results we want. That's because leading alone is exhausting. A team of leaders exponentially multiplies what any one leader can do; when all of us lead, we work on our failures together and all of us get the pleasure of taking credit for our shared success.

What Leaders Crave

We need a team of leaders because as leaders, we crave results. We want more profits if we're in business, we want to help more people if we're in public service, and we want more discoveries if we're in academics—and our desire for more can be an addiction. We're not asking you to give up what you crave. Like chocolate is good, it's only a problem when we eat a whole cake—three nights in a row. If we really want a team of leaders, we have to pay attention to how hard we push—ourselves and our teams—and when. We're quite sure you already know this, and if not, here's the wake-up call: right now, every environment in which we lead is under more pressure than ever before.

In corporate environments, the quest for more is continually grinding down the will of our best people to care about what we do and how we treat our teammates and customers. In academic institutions and nonprofit communities, the competition for scarce dollars is placing all our attention on fund-raising, rather than the missions that inspired us to do our work in the first place. In government, growing deficits and shrinking budgets are forcing every official to spend more time with angry constituents losing their services and less time connecting communities and imagining new worlds. Even our kid's soccer team is feeling more like a professional event, with parents taking the results of the competition as seriously as their favorite pro team.

In the pursuit of results, with our team of leaders, we have to gauge the pressure we're all under. When the pressure is high, we have to be extremely conscious of whether we're following the commitments and giving our fellow leaders the room they need to fulfill them as well. This is why the model itself is so valuable; when we're not paying attention to making three words the script of how we treat one another, something is wrong. And we then immediately know what to do: use the commitments to make sure we've created the environment for success and then support our team of leaders as they apply them to everything they do.

We can each do this every day with some simple exercises. Start every morning with a reflection for yourself: "Do I have clarity, stability, and rhythm today?" If not, ask yourself, "What one thing can I do to fulfill one of the commitments more completely?" Take on your environment next: "What is the one thing I can do to fulfill the three commitments in the place I lead?" Then turn to your most intimate teammates, especially on days when you know the pressure is high. "Do they have clarity, stability, and rhythm?" If not, "What is the one thing I can do to fulfill the commitments with them and create a better experience working together?"

We have to reflect because it is when we raise our consciousness of the three commitments that our teammates can become leaders too. There will be moments when disaster strikes; sometimes we even cause the disaster as leaders. That's when the experience we create for our teammates becomes the most important thing. They'll forgive us our mistakes if they know we're paying attention to them—to what success looks like to them, what they need, and what's getting in their way. When things go wrong and they don't have any hope of clarity, stability, and rhythm, they will never believe as a member of our team of leaders that things can go right. When we constantly try to fulfill the three commitments, our teammates will as well; the results we want, even on the worst days, are always a day closer.

CHAPTER 6

1,000,000 LEADERS

A World of Leaders

What if every human being on the planet could describe the way leaders we want to follow think and act? What if every child, as part of the kindergarten curriculum, was taught the fundamentals of how to lead? What if every time leaders failed us, we knew how to redefine success, ask for what we needed, and, when necessary, become the leaders who discover and implement the ideas of how to fix the problems that inevitably arise in a growing population on a finite globe?

We have a dream for a braver new world: we want a world of leaders. The paralysis facing us in so many geopolitical conflicts, uncertain economies, and struggling communities and organizations in every country is a failure in education about leadership. We hold up the great leaders as heroes and turn them into mythical demigods when, in many cases, any one of us could do what they did if we simply were given the right knowledge early and were supported as we learned the hard lessons that every leader must experience.

What leaders do is not complicated; it is simply difficult. But difficult tasks are the foundation of human evolution. The evolution we want to see, like the first sea creatures finding their legs as they learned to walk on dry earth, is a new consciousness about what it truly means to lead. Too often leadership is confused with management—with the art of getting things done. Leadership is the act of making new realities possible. That's what the three commitments do: they create a new reality.

We want this simple way of thinking to become muscle memory in every child. When a child experiences confusion on a team, we want her to know that it usually happens because everyone on the team is not clear. When a child feels insecure, we want him to know that he can take specific steps to rebuild the stability, which infuses the environment with renewed trust. When a child feels stuck, we want her to not lose a beat before looking for the block in the rhythm that always pops up in a chaotic life in a constantly changing universe.

We want the three commitments to become the foundation of an evolution in the way human beings lead for the future. They are not the ultimate answer to all the troubles of humanity; they are the cornerstones of creating cultures in which we're all focused on alleviating the troubles of humanity. We've been paying attention to the wrong parts of how we live and work together, and what we need to do differently is about spreading the message about how simple the change in thinking needs to be.

Kissing Your Enemy

As we can't build a team of leaders without believing every person can lead, creating entire cultures where others become leaders begins when we treat people in a way that transcends our reactionary emotions under stress and fear, even in the worst circumstances. In the Egyptian revolution of 2011, one of the key leaders was a Google marketing executive, Wael Ghonim. He was instantly held up as an example for the value of social media when gathering people for change. His story as an unintentional leader is also a pivotal example for how we build a world of leaders. He never wanted the role; he experienced the worst of other human beings, and he still treated even his captors with dignity.

Ghonim was arrested as one of the organizers of the protests, culminating in the hundreds of thousands who shut down Cairo's Tahrir Square. After his release from jail, the story he told in an interview on CBS' *60 Minutes* is one of the most profound examples of creating an environment where everyone can lead. He described what he felt and did after being blindfolded, handcuffed, and beaten. He said, "I forgive them, I have to say. I forgive them because . . . they were convinced that I was harming the country." He explains that he was beaten by the soldiers, not the officers who lead them. "These are simple people, not educated . . . For [the soldier], I'm sort of like a traitor. I'm destabilizing the country. So when he hits me, he doesn't hit me because he's a bad guy. He's hitting me because he thinks he's a good guy."

When someone on our team makes a mistake that ruins a deal or slows down our progress, or when one of our neighbors gets angry at a town meeting when his perspective is completely opposite to our own, imagine being this understanding. Even when we're tired or frustrated, every one of us can be so deeply connected to the humanness of the people in our lives that we don't overreact. It matters so much because the way we behave when things are at their worst has everything to do with how others will behave in the future. When Ghonim was freed, what he did is one of the greatest moments leadership history will ever capture: "On the last day, I removed my blindfold, and I said, 'Hi,' and kissed every one of them. All of the soldiers. It was good. I was sending them a message."

Ghonim's kisses sent the world a message. He was not just trying to overthrow a government that was beating its people; he wanted to send a clear message about what needed to happen next. Ghonim, in the way all of us are capable if our minds know what to focus on, hoped for freedom even for the people who wanted the worst for him. As leaders today, our role is not just to see what needs to get done; we have to anticipate, particularly when others can't, environments where all of us have the opportunity for lives of meaning and connection.

On February 8, the crowd started chanting, "One hand, one hand," meaning we are one—that all Egyptians were united. In front of 100,000 people, Ghonim said, "I'm not the hero. I was just typing on my keyboard. You are the heroes." He could have rallied the crowd against the government. He could have instigated extreme violence. Instead, he spoke of unity. He created stability with his words. "This is not a time to settle scores for personal gains, and it's not a time for parties or ideologies. It's time to say one thing: Egypt above all." He urged a new rhythm for every citizen—a life of opportunity where everyone mattered. He didn't call for himself to be the focus of attention; he called them for them to be heard—for a new country, a nation of leaders, where every person has the freedom and fairness they need to play their role—to be leaders as well.

The Math

We need a million people. This is not a pipe dream; the three commitments are a way of making life better for all of us. We believe a million of us can make the commitments, and we need your help. First, go to threecommitments.com and "like" the commitments. It seems as if it's such a simple act, but if we don't actually make the mental move of registering our desire to live this way as leaders, the moment we put this book down, it may become just another good concept that collects cobwebs in our consciousness. This is absolutely our attempt to draw attention to this way of thinking. We absolutely need your help. We ask you to take this first action to prove to yourself you are a leader who wants to take these simple ways of being and make them a daily part of your life.

Now let's imagine: a million people each teach five people the three commitments and then ask them to teach five. If that pattern continues a few more times, starting with the first million, we will only be six degrees of relationship away from the whole world knowing how simple it is to lead. The world population is fast approaching seven billion people. Look at how quickly the commitments could spread exponentially:

 1 to 5
 5 to 25
 25 to 125
 125 to 625
 625 to 3,625
3,625 to more people than perhaps will ever inhabit the world

You talk to five people every day who have leadership roles about the places where they want to see things done better. You may have five people in your family.

Our dream about spreading the three commitments is based on a desire to change the collective consciousness of the globe about leadership. As 2011 brings revolution across countries in Africa and the Middle East, the consciousness of the leaders was raised by what was wrong. What if the same tools of social media that fought police brutality and government corruption could also be used to develop people? We want the pace of leadership development to take a quantum leap. We want the world to know how simple it is to lead so that the kind of revolutions spawned by dictatorships and broken lives can transform into new realities of possibility and communities in which people don't have to be oppressed for generations to build lives in which they have what they need.

Of course, we're assuming we can gather the first million people. Wait, one million people making the three commitments is a huge number. That's going to be so hard to achieve. Yes, but maybe not: the first million will be the easiest million. In the world of social media, we can use the tools to connect to people all around the globe, quickly and in a way that positively changes our lives. We're not asking people to do the really hard stuff like giving up chocolate or cheeseburgers.

We're asking you to make three simple words the way you interact with your colleagues, neighbors, and families. We're asking you to like this way of thinking and click a button. We're asking you to live this way so that others want to learn your secret and you can start their learning with three words.

The Musicians' Village

When we apply the three commitments to the natural disasters that seem to be swallowing our world city by city, suddenly epic pain becomes the seeds of communities being reborn.

When Harry Connick Jr. sat at the piano next to Ellis Marsalis at the New Orleans Center for Creative Arts in the 1970s, New Orleans didn't know it was their piano lessons that would save one of the city's most precious possessions.

When Hurricane Katrina devastated the Crescent City in 2005, the world didn't realize it almost lost the heart of jazz.

Jazz music is one of the clearest examples of a team of leaders working together. But the kind of virtuosity needed to excel at jazz, the kind of team leadership exhibited by the legendary 1950's ensemble The Quintet, is learned in stages: after mastering their chops—the basic notes, instrument technique, and patterns of music—jazz players practice for hours a day with other musicians learning to support one another and take the lead on a piece.

The art is handed from more experienced players to younger students. The life of a jazz musician is not easy and the money is not good. The pleasure is in the playing and the jamming together, the passing on of the classic tunes and the constant innovation of new styles. When the hurricane destroyed the houses and the neighborhoods—the places where the musicians lived so they could gather at night to play—jazz left the city. The music could not return until the musicians had a place to lay their instruments down for the night. Without its musicians, the city almost lost its rhythm.

It was saved by the relationship between Branford Marsalis and Harry Connick Jr., who learned to play with the five Marsalis brothers at the knees of their father, Ellis. Harry Connick Jr. and Branford, the oldest of the five brothers, realized that the clearest action they could take for the city after the storm was to create new homes for their peers. Most had lived in dilapidated housing before the flood, and the dream was to create a village for musicians and their families where the bright-colored houses—orange, purple, yellow, and pink—would surround a performance center. If they wanted to maintain the tradition of New Orleans jazz, they knew that the artists needed stability in their lives to focus on their music. Harry Connick Jr. and Branford Marsalis knew that for the traditions to be passed on as father had to sons, there had to be a life that facilitated the rhythm of teaching and collaboration that produces jazz greatness.

The fund-raising began after Katrina; in conjunction with Habitat for Humanity, they began to build 72 single-family homes on eight acres of land in the Ninth Ward, the part of the city most affected by the hurricane. They were clear on their goal: save jazz. They knew the stability that was needed: homes. They built a rhythm of effort in which volunteers from around the world came to hammer the pieces of a shattered culture back together, room by room and family by family. The houses are now complete and by fall 2011, the Ellis Marsalis Center for Music will open in the center of the neighborhood, complete with a 150-person auditorium, classrooms, and the administrative support young musicians need to focus on their music as a way of life.

The music passed from Ellis Marsalis to his sons and others then became leadership passed from them to a world that would build the Musicians' Village. This is the way a world of leadership spreads. The enthusiasm of a few passes on as they make the three commitments and then the way they lead infects everyone who touches projects such as the Musicians' Village. And the energy doesn't stop flowing once the project is done. The story travels with every person who visits, goes there to see a concert, or reads about it. Every note that comes out of the neighborhood will continue the rebuilding of a community and the building of a world of leaders.

Leaders for Life

Once we become leaders, it is not something we stop doing. Leaders never retire. We change venues, but we never stop leading. The reason we want our children educated in this way of thinking and prioritizing how they work with others emerges from a problematic Western attitude toward progress, and ultimately, the human race: too many of us are doing what we do so we can stop.

In business, fueled by the Internet boom of the 1990s and the beginning of the first decade of the new millennium, starting a company has too often become about selling it so we can stop and retire on an island. Winning an election is about the victory and gaining the position of power, not how to use the office as one opportunity in a life of helping others. We want the position, the best seller, or the deal so we can have the wealth to stop, but serious success is actually the moment that our impact as people truly begins.

The desire for total freedom is completely natural, but it's simply not the attitude of a leader. When we really lead, we always look for the ways we can create lasting experiences that truly make other's lives better. The three commitments create the kind of personal attention to what it means to lead so that leadership becomes a part of our DNA every day, at every stage of life.

The day that Aaron Feuerstein turned 70 years old, on December 11, 1995, his company burned to the ground. Malden Mills, the original creator of Polartec, was a $400 million dollar company that had just expanded with a trajectory to be a billion dollar firm by the turn of the twenty-first century. As Feuerstein—a third generation owner—celebrated his birthday with friends and family, an explosion rocked one of the factories, ultimately destroying three of nine buildings at the company's Lawrence, Massachusetts factory.

Feuerstein is still considered one of the ultimate case studies in ethical leadership. He could have taken hundreds of millions in insurance money and moved on. He could have moved his factory overseas. He certainly didn't have to maintain the $1.5-million-a-week payroll obligations as the factory was rebuilt. Instead, he kept 3,000 employees on the payroll—costing him $25 million. He made a clear commitment to maintain the stability of his people in a time where they lost all their normal rhythm. The company eventually needed to file for Chapter 11 bankruptcy in 2001, but he never wavered in the clarity of what he was doing and why, the stability he wanted to retain for his team and the Lawrence community, and the rhythm of life he wanted to return to his organization.

With his team of leaders, he ultimately brought the company back to its previous heights, including a $16 million contract with the U.S. Department of Defense. Feuerstein actually lost control of the company to creditors with the 2001 bankruptcy but kept his presidency and position as chairman of the board. He resigned from those posts in 2004 to try to repurchase his legacy. As the leadership began shipping jobs overseas, he was committed to his people. The company filed for bankruptcy again in 2007 and has since been sold. Almost sounds like Feuerstein failed.

But that's not the end of the story. A group of employees who Feuerstein believed in throughout the years opened Mill Direct Textiles, in Lawrence. As Feuerstein continued to fight for his employees, his living the three commitments translated into a team of leaders who is now continuing his legacy. In addition to dollars and cents, we measure leaders in lives changed, ideas generated, and the legacy they inspire. Leadership is not something we do for a while and then because we have some good results, we go to Disneyland. Leadership is a way of life that at its highest level infects others with the capacity and courage to lead too.

The conclusion to the story of Malden Mills is even better than Feuerstein's always paying attention to what his teams needed or the team of leaders he inspired to create Mill Direct. The city of Lawrence was renewed. Buildings that had been empty for decades filled with businesses and homes. The mall that had been empty since the early 1990s is now being rebuilt as a health and technology education center for the local community college. Crime has dropped and still remained below peak levels, with increases due to the global recession of 2008. The downtown shopping district, a ghost town since the 1970s, is open for business. Are all these improvements a result of the lifetime leadership of Feuerstein? Of course not. They are a result of the places in which he created clarity, stability, and rhythm—and a city of leaders that continues to reemerge.

A Community of Aspiration

The three commitments is a philosophy of aspiration. To aspire is to soar. It's to have a vision that leaps beyond the horizon we can see and yet is grounded in a confidence that knows that new realities can come into being. The problem with most world-changing leaders is that we do not have enough fellow leaders around us to support the work we're doing. No matter how great our team of leaders and no matter how grounded we are as people, every single one of us who takes up the mantle of leadership goes stale sometimes. We go dry because we give everything we have. What we need are communities of leaders who surround us with the kind of stimulation that revives our desire to lead in the places where the world simply isn't complete without us.

Where do you go when your well is dry? Let's assume that you pay attention to your personal renewal, and you have a rhythm that keeps your body and mind healthy. The way we can lead for our whole lives is to stay in touch with a community of leaders who push us when we want to quit, keep us accountable to what it means to lead well, and constantly challenge us with new ways to lead effectively. There is no "proper" community that will fill this need for you, just like there is no absolute way to fulfill the three commitments. But there are types of communities that will fuel your ability to be the leadership giant the world needs you to be.

The first category is colleague groups. Whether you are an executive who has a CEO roundtable or a professional—such as a doctor, lawyer, teacher, or minister—who has a regular practice group that explores the best ways to live out your vocation, you need people who will value your desire to lead and keep you honest about whether you're living up to your potential as a leader. Don't choose a group just because they are in your town or you do the same thing. You want a group of people who will move you: we have to want to attend the group, respect every member deeply, and be willing to open ourselves to the group so we can truly learn. With the advent of social media, we can form these groups around the world and meet in ways that simply weren't possible even a few years ago. Our only limitation in finding the right colleagues to help us keep our three commitments is our level of willingness to find them.

A second category is community centers. In every city and town there are faith communities, YMCAs, and art centers where we can be deeply moved by committed volunteers, thinkers, and creative human beings who love to share what they do. We all need a community like the Artists Collective in

Hartford, Connecticut. Begun in the 1970s in borrowed buildings around the city, its classrooms and stages today promote the music, dance, and drama of the African diaspora.

Visit the center, and as you walk the halls you will not only be amazed by the energy of the students, you will quickly grasp that every staff member—from the executive director to the custodian—not only feels empowered to lead, they also know exactly what they do, why they do it, and what Artists Collective stands for. As leaders, when we walk into a community center that knows its mission and passes its purpose on to every person who walks through its doors, as leaders we can't help but soak up the vibe and find new ways to fulfill the three commitments.

A third category is conferences. When you sit around a table with colleagues who face the same issues, you very quickly realize you are not the only leader who has that unique challenge. The problems most of us face aren't unique. The classic methods of solving problems may sometimes evolve slowly. What's unique are the ways we will employ tested solutions, and the creative ideas we need emerge only when we have teammates with whom we can craft the next solutions. Be thoughtful about the conferences you choose, because many can be as much about business as they are about connecting leaders in different disciplines and around powerful ideas. And conferences can be the retreat every leader needs to connect with a community of leaders who care just as much about the world we're trying to build.

These are the obvious places to look for a community of leaders. Ask yourself, "Where will I go to find the support, energy, and insight I need to never stop leading?" We want a million leaders because we want communities of aspiration in every town and city, in every state and province. We want teams of leaders in the places we lead, and communities of aspiration that connect us to the ways each of us can stay inspired. We need one another. The three commitments are a way of thinking about leadership that starts conversations among those of us who lead. The infinite ways to fulfill them change each day and with each new revolution of our world. It is in communities of fellow leaders that we will find the energy to never stop leading.

The Inevitable Doubt

We need communities of aspiration because the risks of leadership are real. The moment when the leadership enthusiasm goes from words to actions, it's not that we don't know what we have to do—the three commitments show us where we need to focus our attention—but the problem is that we may wonder if the risks are worth it.

In Martin Luther King Jr.'s memoir, *Stride Toward Freedom*, he recounts the story of 50,000 fellow civil rights leaders boycotting the segregated buses over two years. On the night of January 27, 1956, over a year into the struggle, he wondered if he should quit. His phone rang just as he was falling asleep. The voice said, "Before next week you'll be sorry you ever came to Montgomery." After making coffee and hours of pacing, with his mind filled with dark thoughts and doubts, he sat at the kitchen table with his head in his hands.

He knew every day that his life and his family's lives were in danger. Did the need for a leader justify the potential cost? Being a leader, whether we're in a movement or an organization, is not safe. Whatever we are called to build or change or renew, there will be those who will oppose us. In some cases, they oppose us because they too think they are fighting for what is right. On King's deep, dark night, he described hearing a voice. He told the story in a sermon a year later, he knew he had to "Stand up for the truth. Stand up for righteousness." Despite the real danger he knew was coming, he could not let the world exist as it did at that moment.

Three days later, his house was bombed. Sometimes a leader who makes it possible for the whole world to lead has to be able to face even bombs. King stood before a crowd of hundreds and assured them he and his family were fine. Notice the clarity with which he spoke. He immediately created stability with his calm voice and said:

Don't get panicky. Don't do anything panicky. Don't get your weapons. If you have weapons, take them home. He who lives by the sword will perish by the sword. Remember that is what Jesus said. We are not advocating violence. We want to love our enemies. I want you to love our enemies. Be good to them. This is what we must live by. We must meet hate with love.

He paused when the crowd got noisy. He created a rhythm with his words that modeled the nonviolent protest. He wouldn't let those that wanted to derail the future tens of thousands in Montgomery knew could happen—a future of freedom and equal opportunity—with a few careless acts of violence. He continued:

I did not start this boycott. I was asked by you to serve as your spokesman. I want it to be known the length and breadth of this land that if I am stopped, this movement will not stop. If I am stopped, our work will not stop. For what we are doing is right. What we are doing is just. And God is with us.

The movement could have ended with the riots. The power of the civil rights struggle was the nonviolent way it emphasized the unspeakable wrongs being done to people based only on skin color. A break in that model would destroy the power of its purpose. Even though he doubted, even though he faced unbelievable risks that ultimately took his life, the way King spoke, the way he lead, created an environment in which instead of the movement's dying, it thrived. Because he led, millions became leaders too.

Lead Every Day

We don't lead just because we're the CEO of a corporation or the coach of a professional team. We lead everywhere, and we lead every day. Some of us lead at home and others in our communities. We don't have to be elected to Congress or earn the big promotion; to lead, we simply have to want to help new and better realities come into being. What's better to you is the place where you have leadership worth doing.

We keep the momentum of our leadership going day after day by paying attention to where we lead. The method we have to use each day as leaders is too rarely a part of our lives: reflection. We talk to too many leaders who have so many good ideas, but caught in the landslide of their desire to be great at everything they do, they never stop. As we've asked you to reflect on all three commitments, we want to finish the book building a new ritual for your daily life.

At the end of each day, ask yourself two questions. First: *where did you lead today?* Where did you take the three commitments seriously and apply them to the real challenges and dreams of your daily life? Fulfilling the three commitments and making them a way of living for the people around you so they can lead too doesn't have to come with giant plans and complicated infrastructure. Who did you speak with in a way that shared knowledge and helped someone else find clarity? Where did you build a little more stability through the resources you provided and the trust you inspired? There is absolutely some place in the past 24 hours where you paid attention to the flow of your team's work and to the timing of how you lead. Where did you build that new world?

Second, and this may be the simplest way to build a team of leaders around you: *where did you compliment someone else for leading?* As we all run with our heads down when we make mistakes, we're not just scraping our knees. The leadership failures in our world today are more akin to pushing entire buildings of people off a cliff: Enron, Lehman Brothers, and Bear Stearns; Egypt, Syria, Haiti, and Libya. We don't have to look far to see how difficult and precarious our interconnected world is and how dangerous poor leadership is—that's why when we notice great leadership happening around us, we have to say so.

On one of our retreats while writing this book, we were at a hotel with a conference of U.S. military officers. We noticed the way they interacted with one another and every stranger they met. As we took an elevator with one of the leaders, we commented on how impressed we were with the way they conducted themselves, and that their behavior was clearly a reflection of the group's strong leadership. The next day, as we sat writing in the lobby, the master sergeant heading the group sought us out. He presented us with a medal.

He wanted to thank us for noticing what they were trying to accomplish. He had told the story to all his officers and it had reinforced how important the work they were doing could be. The story sounds absurd: a medal from a member of our military, given to a civilian just for paying attention? But the master sergeant was actually emphasizing the importance of noticing the efforts of others' leadership. If we're leaders, when we walk into the room, everyone looks at us. They look up to us. They need us. We are always leading every day and it matters in every moment.

The question is, are we up to it? Do you have the courage to fulfill the three commitments every day, to build a team of leaders, in fact, a world of people ready to evolve the human race into a new level of creative possibility? If we do not pour ourselves into developing teams of leaders as intently as we pay attention to the core activities of what we do—such as finance, product development, and talent management—we will run out of energy. We can't run our governments, businesses, and communities without a team of leaders so vast that when our bodies and minds need to pause, there are able teammates just as ready as we were to take the lead.

If we're up to it, we, the leaders—whether we have the authority yet or we are the ones with the kernel of a dream—can turn every company and country, every individual and team, every single community into a place where people have the clarity, stability, and rhythm to live lives of true happiness. The three commitments are about improving performance and helping organizations increase their results; perhaps the greatest result we can hope for is a world where the things that separate us as people become the opportunities to apply the three commitments and rebuild a world of leaders where each of us has what we want, need, and love.

Postlude: The Unexpected Prize

You are a leader. You have a team. You run an organization. There is a moment that can make all the pain and struggle of leadership worth it. Someone calls you up after a few years, sometimes even after a few decades. You were his boss at his first job or his coach in high school. You might have been his spiritual leader or the government official who took his call. He says, "I really need us to get together." Because you take leadership seriously every day, when someone says it's important that you meet, the alarm in your brain goes off. You start to imagine what's wrong, because that's too often what your life is about—fixing problems—and you wonder why he's calling you.

You ask if there is something you can do for him now, and he says no. He tells you where to meet him. It's a good restaurant around the corner from your office. When you arrive, he is already waiting. He looks at you with a smile that would soften the hardest heart and make the grumpiest day worth enduring. You sit down, and he tells you why he wanted to see you.

The person just wants to say thank you.

He wants to say thank you because you were the leader who paid attention. You saw the potential in each teammate and you nurtured it. You created an environment where people wanted to work together—where teammates made each other better, felt free to challenge what was being done, and take risks to improve the work. You had the courage to take on the real needs that most people ignored, not knowing what to do. He noticed, and he wants you to know your leadership had an impact.

And there is a second unexpected moment in leadership, a prize that few of us have been taught is possible. This is what you will make happen when you fulfill the three commitments everywhere you lead. As leaders we can create the environment through our actions in which every person on our team can become a leader too. The ultimate result of the three commitments is not just your leadership acuity; it's your ability to develop a team of leaders. If we do, when they take us out to dinner, it won't be just to thank us for our leadership, it will be for supporting them in becoming the leaders they always wanted to be.

SELECTED
BIBLIOGRAPHY

Aurelius, Marcus. *Meditations*. Book II. George Long translation. http://classics.mit.edu/.

Bracha, Stefan H. "Does 'Fight or Flight' Need Updating?" *Psychosomatics* 45 (October 2004): 448–449.

Bradford, Sarah Hopkins. *Harriet, the Moses of Her People*. New York: Geo. R. Lockwood and Son, 1897.

Branch, Taylor. *Parting the Water: America in the King Years, 1954-63*. New York: Simon & Schuster, 1988.

Clary, David A. *Rocket Man: Robert H. Goddard and the Birth of the Space Age*. New York: Hyperion, 2003.

Csikszentmihalyi, Mihaly. *Flow: The Psychology of Optimal Experience*. New York: Harper & Row, Inc., 1990.

Dante. *Comedy*. Canto xxi. Longfellow, H.W. translation. Dante.ilt.columbia.edu/comedy.

Davis, Robert C. *Shipbuilders of the Venetian Arsenal: Workers and Workplace in the Preindustrial City*. Baltimore, MD: Johns Hopkins University Press, 2007.

Ford, Henry and Samuel Crowther. *Edison as I Know Him*. New York: Cosmopolitan Book Corporation, 1930.

Gilbert, Daniel. *Stumbling on Happiness*. New York: Alfred A. Knopf, 2006.

Gruver, Ed. "The Lombardi Sweep: The Signature Play of the Green Bay Dynasty, It Symbolized an Era." *The Coffin Corner*: 19, no. 5 (1997).

Hampton, Brad and Kim Hampton. "John F. Kennedy's True Love." Yachtpals.com. October 21, 2010.

Hersey, John. "Survival." *The New Yorker*, June 17, 1944.

King Jr., Martin Luther. *Stride Towards Freedom: The Montgomery Story*. New York: Harper & Brothers, 1958.

Malina, Frank, J. "The Rocket Pioneers." *Engineering & Science*, November 1986, 8–13.

Mallinger, Mark and Gerry Rossy. "The Trader Joe's Experience: The Impact of Corporate Culture on Business Strategy." *Graziadio Business Report* 10, issue 2 (2007).

Maslow, Abraham. "A Theory of Human Motivation." *Psychological Review* 50, no. 4 (1943): 370–396.

Salter, Chuck. "Whirlpool Finds Its Cool." *Fast Company*, June 1, 2005.

Seligman, Martin. *Authentic Happiness: Using the New Positive Psychology to Realize Your Potential for Lasting Fulfillment*. New York: The Free Press, 2002.

Shackleton, Ernest. *In the Heart of the Antarctic: The Furthest South Expedition*. London: Heineman, 1909.

Shackleton, E. R. "Some Results of the British Antarctic Expedition, 1907-1909." *Annual Report of the Board of Regents of the Smithsonian Institution, 1909*. Washington: Government Printing Office, 1910.

Swartz, Barry. *The Paradox of Choice: Why Less is More*. New York: Harper Collins, 2004.

Welch, Jack and John Byrne. *Jack: Straight from the Gut*. New York: Warner Books, Inc., 2001.

INDEX

Acting to create new realities, 8–13
Action plan, clarity, 17–18
Activities you love, rhythm, 114–115
Add, keep, delete (clarity), 45–48
Alarm, stability, 83–84
Amazon.com, 90–91
Anger, respond with magnanimity, 104
Anthony, Susan B., 159
Artists Collective, Hartford, CT,
    178–179
Asking questions (*see* Questions to ask)
Assessment:
    blocks to rhythm, 139–140
    of needs, stability, 105–107
    of readiness, building leaders,
        154–155
    for success, clarity, 16, 66–68
Attention, clarity, 48–50
Aurelius, Marcus, 157–158
Awareness, and stability, 28

Bad news, and trust, 104–105
Bane, John, 64
Blind men baking bread analogy, clarity,
    38–39
Brain:
    and clarity, 50–54
    happiness and rhythm, 124–127
Building a team of leaders (*see* Leaders,
    building team of)

Cadence, and rhythm, 134
Caring about your team, 102–104
Cause, energy needed for action, 14–15

Choice:
    as foundation of rhythm, 123–124
    offering to people who are stuck, 105
Chores of life, stability, 87–88
Circadian rhythms, 111
Clarity, 35–68
    action plan, 17–18
    add, keep, delete, 45–48
    addressing underperformers ("Jack"),
        20, 22–28
    as assessment for success, 16, 66–68
    blind men baking bread analogy,
        38–39
    commitment to, described, 35–38
    Thomas Edison, 121
    Five Whys, 54–56
    How do you define success?, 61–62
    John F. Kennedy, 3
    leader aspirations, 9–10
    in meetings, 31
    paying attention, 48–50
    possession of, 39–41
    puzzle pieces, 56–65
    questions to ask, 40–41, 54–65
    reframing, 65–66
    sponge and shortcuts, 50–54
    Harriet Tubman, 42–45, 107
    What do I want?, 40
    What need do you satisfy?, 59–61
    What values govern your actions?,
        62–64
    Where do you communicate the
        messages everyone needs?,
        64–65

Who is your customer?, 58–59
Why?, 54–56
Why do I lead?, 41
Why is the place where I'm leading important?, 41
Coaching, as needs, 73
Colleague groups, in leadership community, 178
Commitments:
    applying to current situations, 15–20
    leader aspirations, 9–13
    (*See also* Clarity; Rhythm; Stability)
Communication:
    reframing, clarity, 65–66
    stability, 90–91
    (*See also* Questions to ask)
Community centers, in leadership community, 178–179
Community of aspiration, leadership, 177–180
Conferences, in leadership community, 179
Confident leader development, 159–162
Connections and interactions, rhythm, 117
Connick, Harry Jr., 172–174
Core motivation to lead (asking why), 156–159
Cravings, from leaders, 165–166
Create new realities, 8–13
Creating culture of stability, 96–102
Csikszentmihalyi, Mihaly, 125
Culture of stability:
    creating, 96–102
    defined, 72
    starting, 72–74

Daily leadership, 182–184
Dante, 109–110
Desire needed to build leaders, 154–155
Development plan:
    clarity, 18–19
    culture of trust, 96–99
    rhythm, 29
Doubt, leaders, 180–182
Douglass, Frederick, 158–159
Drills, tactical, 100–102

Edison, Thomas, 118–123
Egyptian 2011 uprising, 169–170
Elephant approach, to build leaders, 149–154

Emotions:
    stability, 84–86, 102–105
    transcending reactionary, 168–170
End of the day, rhythm, 115–116
Enemy, kissing your, 168–170
Energy, rhythm, 115, 136–137
Eris, Greek goddess of confusion, 35–36, 66

Fear response recognition, stability, 84–86
Feuerstein, Aaron, 175–177
Five Whys, 54–56
Flat leadership, 147–148
Flow: The Psychology of Optimal Experience (Csikszentmihalyi), 125
Fluency, to build leaders, 154–155
Food, as needs, 73
Ford, Henry, 118–123
Forest and trees, rhythm, 139–140
Free lunch, Hospital for Special Care, 86–87
Freeedom as foundation of rhythm, 123–124
Friendship, as needs, 73
Functional level, rhythm, 129–131

General Electric, 62–63
General Mills, 91–94
Ghonim, Wael, 169–170
Gilbert, Daniel, 126
Gillespie, Dizzy, 148
Goddard, Robert, 141–144
Google, 169–170
Green Bay Packers, 100–101

Happiness and rhythm, 124–127
Harlow, Harry, 69
Heuristics, 53
Hierarchical leadership, 147–148
Honesty, clarity questions, 55–56
Hospital for Special Care, Connecticut, 86–87
How do you define success?, 61–62
Hsieh, Tony, 89

Inferno (Dante), 109–110
Innovation mentor program, Whirlpool, 133
Inspiration level, rhythm, 131–132

Jazz:
   Massey Hall concert, Toronto
      (1953), 148–149
   in post-Katrina New Orleans,
      172–174

Kármán, Theodore von, 143–144
Kennedy, Joe, 33
Kennedy, John F., 1–8, 137–138
King, Martin Luther Jr., 180–182
Kissing your enemy, 168–170

Layoffs, 99–100
Leader aspirations, 1–33
   acting to create new realities, 8–13
   addressing underperformers, 20–33
   applying the commitments now,
      15–20
   clarity, 9–10
   commitments, 9–13
   John F. Kennedy, 1–8
   learning to be a leader, 13–15
   rhythm, 11–12
   stability, 10–11
Leaders, building team of, 141–166
   confident leader development,
      159–162
   core motivation to lead (asking why),
      156–159
   described, 147–149
   elephant approach, 149–154
   fluency, 154–155
   Robert Goddard, 141–144
   opportunities, 144–147
   readiness assessment, 154–155
   resiliency, 154–155
   show the candidate their potential,
      160
   surrounding us, 162–164
   talk about how you lead, 160–161
   talk about your mistakes, 161–162
   as ultimate prize, 185–186
   what leaders crave, 165–166
   will and desire, 154–155
Leaders, world of, 167–186
   community of aspiration, 177–180
   Harry Connick Jr. and Branford
      Marsalis, 172–174
   daily leadership, 182–184
   difficulty of leadership, 168
   doubt, 180–182
   kissing your enemy, 168–170

lifelong, 174–177
a million people to change the world,
   170–172
transcending reactionary emotions,
   168–170
unexpected prize, 184–186
Leadership:
   building team of leaders, 141–166
   clarity, 35–68
   leader aspirations, 1–33
   learning to be a leader, 13–15
   models of, 147–148
   rhythm, 109–140
   stability, 69–107
   world of leaders, 167–186
Learning unlimited, stability, 88–89
Lego, 131–132
Lifelong leaders, 174–177
Lindbergh, Charles, 143
Lombardi, Vince, 100–101

Machiavelli, Niccolò, 157
Malden Mills, Lawrence, MA, 175–177
Mandela, Nelson, 159
Mantras, 53
Marsalis, Branford, 173–174
Marsalis, Ellis, 172–173
Maslow, Abraham, 69–72, 125
Meaning, and happiness, 126
Measurement, rhythm, 127–134
Meditations (Aurelius), 157
Meetings, 31
Mill Direct, Lawrence, MA, 176–177
A million people to change the world,
   170–172
Mingus, Charlie, 148
Mistakes:
   talk about, to build leaders, 161–162
   transcending reactionary emotions,
      169–170
Mornings, rhythm, 114
Motorola USA, 130

Needs:
   simple assessment of needs, 105–107
   What need do you satisfy?, 59–61
   Where do you communicate the
      messages everyone needs?,
      64–65
New Orleans, jazz in post-Katrina,
   172–174
New realities, creating, 8–13

New York Times, 142
Nimrod and Ernest Shackelton, 76–82, 107
Notice your team, 102–104

Olds, Ransom, 110
Opportunities, to build leaders, 144–147
Organization of work, rhythm, 111

The Paradox of Choice (Schwartz), 123
Parker, Charlie, 148
Patterns of rhythm, 117–118
Paying attention, clarity, 48–50
People, and the bottom line, 128
Perfect work day, rhythm, 113–116
Possession of stability, 75–76
Potential, show the candidate their, to build leaders, 160
Praise, as needs, 74
Pressure, on leaders, 165–166
Profiling, 53
Puzzle pieces, clarity, 56–65

Questions to ask:
    clarity, 40–41, 54–65
    Five Whys, 54–56
    How do you define success?, 61–62
    What do I want?, 24, 40
    What need do you satisfy?, 59–61
    What needs work? as weekly review question, 135
    What values govern your actions?, 62–64
    What went well? as weekly review question, 135
    When did you compliment someone else for leading?, 183–184
    Where did you lead today?, 182–183
    Where do you communicate the messages everyone needs?, 64–65
    Who is your customer?, 58–59
    Why?, 54–56, 156–159
    Why do I lead?, 41
    Why is the place where I'm leading important?, 24, 41

Radar, stability, 83–84
Readiness assessment, to build leaders, 154–155
Reframing, clarity, 65–66
Regular updates, culture of trust, 99–100

Resiliency, to build leaders, 154–155
Resources for success, and stability, 75
Results, as leader goal, 165–166
Rhythm, 109–140
    action plan, 17–18
    addressing underperformers ("Jack"), 20
    as assessment, 16
    commitment to, described, 109–113
    Thomas Edison, 118–123
    Henry Ford, 118–123
    freeedom as foundation of, 123–124
    happiness and, 124–127
    imagine the perfect work day, 113–116
    John F. Kennedy, 5
    leader aspirations, 11–12
    maintaining, 138–139
    measurement, 127–134
    in meetings, 31–32
    possession of, 116–118
    ritual renewal, 136–139
    simple assessment on blocks to, 139–140
    timing, 111
    Venetian Arsenal, 109–110
    weekly review, 134–136
Ritual renewal, rhythm, 136–139
Rocket to the moon, Robert Goddard, 141–144
Routines, effectiveness, rhythm, 116–117
Rutledge, Matt, 90–91

Schwartz, Barry, 123
Scott, Robert, 77
Seligman, Martin, 125–126
Shackelton, Ernest and the *Nimrod*, 76–82, 107
Shortcuts and clarity, 50–54
Show the candidate their potential, to build leaders, 160
Similar interests, as needs, 73–74
Sinking ship scenario and John F. Kennedy, 1–8
Six Sigma, 130–131
Sponge and clarity, 50–54
Stability, 69–107
    action plan, 17–18
    addressing underperformers ("Jack"), 28–31
    as assessment, 16
    commitment to, described, 69–72

communication at Zappos and Woot,
  90–91
creating culture of, 96–102
Thomas Edison, 119–121
emotion, 102–105
fear response recognition, 84–86
free lunch, Hospital for Special Care,
  86–87
General Mills, 91–94
John F. Kennedy, 4–5
leader aspirations, 10–11
Maslow on, 69–72
in meetings, 31–32
possession of, 75–76
radar and alarm, 83–84
Ernest Shackelton, 76–82, 107
simple assessment of needs, 105–107
starting culture of, 72–74
taking away the chores of life, 87–88
trust as essential to, 71, 94–96
unlimited learning, 88–89
Starting culture of stability, 72–74
Stride Toward Freedom (King), 180
Stumbling on Happiness (Gilbert), 126
Surrounding us, to build leaders,
  162–164

Tactical drills, 100–102
Taking away the chores of life, stability,
  87–88
Talk about how you lead, to build
  leaders, 160–161
Talk about your mistakes, to build
  leaders, 161–162
Team interactions, rhythm, 111
Team of leaders (*see* Leaders, building
  team of)
"A Theory of Human Motivation"
  (Maslow), 69–70
Three commitments:
  applying to current situations, 15–20
  leader aspirations, 9–13
  (*See also* Clarity; Rhythm; Stability)
Timing and rhythm, 111

Toyota, 54
Trader Joe's, 58–59, 62–64
Trust:
  as essential to stability, 71, 94–96
  and stability, 75–76
Tubman, Harriet, 42–45, 107

Underperformers, addressing, 20–33
Unlimited learning, stability, 88–89

Venetian Arsenal, 109–110

Washington, George, 158
Weekly review, rhythm, 134–136
Welch, Jack, 61–64
What do I want?, 24, 40
What need do you satisfy?, 59–61
What needs work? as weekly review
  question, 135
What values govern your actions?,
  62–64
What went well? as weekly review
  question, 135
When did you compliment someone
  else for leading?, 183–184
Where did you lead today?, 182–183
Where do you communicate the
  messages everyone needs?, 64–65
Whirlpool, 133
Who is your customer?, 58–59
Why?:
  clarity, 54–56
  core motivation to lead, 156–159
Why do I lead?, 41
Why is the place where I'm leading
  important?, 24, 41
Will needed to build leaders, 154–155
Woot.com, 90–91
World of leaders (*see* Leaders,
  world of)

Xerox, 129–130

Zappos, 60–62, 90–91

ABOUT THE AUTHORS

Tom Endersbe has worked for three Fortune 500 firms and been ranked number one nationally as a sales performer and senior leader.

Jay Therrien is a learning expert who has led training and development at three Fortune 500 firms.

Jon Wortmann is a nonprofit leader, coauthor of *Mastering Communication at Work*, and author of the e-book *The Best Communicator in the World*.